Frommer's

Edin...

SHO...

day BY day™

2nd Edition

WITHDRAWN

by Barry Shelby

WILEY

John Wiley & Sons, Inc.

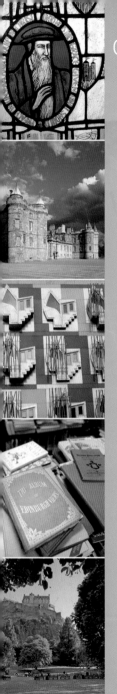

Contents

Editorial...
Production Manager: Daniel Mersey
Commissioning Editor: ...
Development Editor: Jill Emery
Project Editor: Hannah Clement
Photo Research: Cherie Cincilla, Richard H. Fox, Jill Emery
Cartography: Andrew Murphy

Wiley publishes in a variety of print and electronic formats and by print-on-
demand. Some material included with standard print versions of this book
may not be included in e-books or in print-on-demand. If this book refers to
media such as a CD or DVD that is not included in the version you purchased, you may download this material at http://booksupport.wiley.com. .
For more information about Wiley products, visit www.wiley.com.

British Library Cataloguing in Publication Data
A catalogue record for this book is available from the British Library

ISBN 978-1-119-99303-2 (pbk), ISBN 978-1-119-97263-1 (ebk),
ISBN 978-1-119-99473-2 (ebk), ISBN 978-1-119-99456-5 (ebk)

Typeset by Wiley Indianapolis Composition Services
Printed and bound in China by RR Donnelley

5 4 3 2 1

A Note from the Editorial Director

Organizing your time. That's what this guide is all about.

Other guides give you long lists of things to see and do and then expect you to fit the pieces together. The Day by Day guides are different. These guides tell you the best of everything, and then they show you how to see it *in the smartest, most time-efficient way*. Our authors have designed detailed itineraries organized by time, neighborhood, or special interest. And each tour comes with a bulleted map that takes you from stop to stop.

Visitors will find plenty to fill their days: seeking out Mackintosh's architectural gems or rummaging for collectables in the Barras Market of Glasgow, to exploring literary Edinburgh, or climbing up to Arthur's Seat for breathtaking views. Whatever your interest or schedule, the Day by Days give you the smartest routes to follow. Not only do we take you to the top attractions, hotels, and restaurants, but we also help you access those special moments that locals get to experience—those "finds" that turn tourists into travelers.

The Day by Days are also your top choice if you're looking for one complete guide for all your travel needs. The best hotels and restaurants for every budget, the greatest shopping values, the wildest nightlife—it's all here.

Why should you trust our judgment? Because our authors personally visit each place they write about. They're an independent lot who say what they think and would never include places they wouldn't recommend to their best friends. They're also open to suggestions from readers. If you'd like to contact them, please send your comments our way at feedback@frommers.com, and we'll pass them on.

Enjoy your Day by Day guide—the most helpful travel companion you can buy. And have the trip of a lifetime.

Warm regards,

Kelly Regan

Kelly Regan, Editorial Director
Frommer's Travel Guides

About the Author

Barry Shelby was born in 1960 in Berkeley, California, where he later attended the University of California. He moved to Scotland in 1997, where he has worked as a caretaker for a small and privately-owned castle on the Clyde Coast, as a 'temp' with the privatized national railway company, and as a food and drink writer and editor for newspapers and magazines, including the *Guardian*, *Glasgow Herald*, and *The List*. He is married to a Scot and presently resides in Scotland's Western Isles after a decade living in Glasgow.

Acknowledgments

The editor would like to thank Claudia Monteiro at Festivals Edinburgh for her help compiling tip boxes on the Edinburgh Festival (see Chapter 8, p. 95, and Savvy Traveler, p. 165).

Advisory & Disclaimer

Star Ratings, Icons & Abbreviations

Every hotel, restaurant, and attraction listing in this guide has been ranked for quality, value, service, amenities, and special features using a **star-rating system.** Hotels, restaurants, attractions, shopping, and nightlife are rated on a scale of zero stars (recommended) to three stars (exceptional). In addition to the star-rating system, we also use a **kids icon** to point out the best bets for families. Within each tour, we recommend cafes, bars, or restaurants where you can take a break with a £ sign to indicate price. Each of these stops appears in a shaded box marked with a coffee-cup-shaped bullet .

The following **abbreviations** are used for credit cards:

AE	American Express	DISC	Discover	V	Visa
DC	Diners Club	MC	MasterCard		

Travel Resources at Frommers.com

Frommer's travel resources don't end with this guide. Frommer's website, **www.frommers.com**, has travel information on more than 4,000 destinations. We update features regularly, giving you access to the most current trip-planning information and the best airfare, lodging, and car-rental bargains. You can also listen to podcasts, connect with other Frommers.com members through our active-reader forums, share your travel photos, read blogs from guidebook editors and fellow travelers, and much more.

How to Contact Us

In researching this book, we discovered many wonderful places—hotels, restaurants, shops, and more. We're sure you'll find others. Please tell us about them, so we can share the information with your fellow travelers in upcoming editions. If you were disappointed with a recommendation, we'd love to know that, too. Please e-mail: frommers@wiley.com or write to:

Frommer's Edinburgh & the Best of Glasgow Day by Day, 2nd Edition
John Wiley & Sons, Inc. • 111 River St. • Hoboken, NJ 07030-5774

16 Favorite
Moments

16 Favorite **Moments**

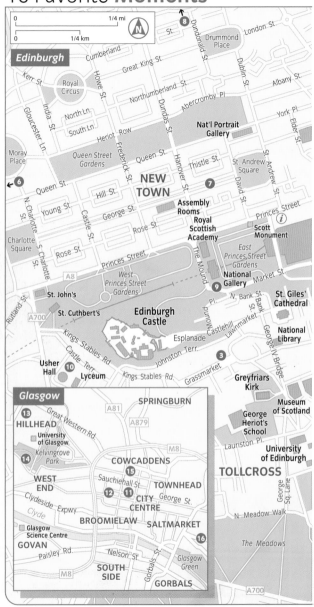

Edinburgh

0 — 1/4 mi
0 — 1/4 km

London St.

Drummond Place

Dundonald St.

Cumberland St.

Great King St.

Dublin St.

Albany St.

Kerr St.

Royal Circus

Howe St.

Northumberland St.

Abercromby Pl.

York Pl.

India St.

North Ln.

South Ln.

Heriot Row

Frederick St.

Queen St.

Dundas St.

Nat'l Portrait Gallery

Elder St.

Gloucester Ln.

Moray Place

Queen Street Gardens

Thistle St.

St. Andrew Square

Queen St.

← 6

Hill St.

NEW TOWN

Hanover St.

7

David St.

St. Andrew St.

N. Charlotte St.

Young St.

George St.

Assembly Rooms

Princes Street

Charlotte Square

Castle St.

Rose St.

Royal Scottish Academy

Scott Monument

ⓘ

S. Charlotte St.

Rose St.

Princes Street

West Princes Street Gardens

The Mound

East Princes Street Gardens

Market St.

A8

National Gallery

9

N. Bank St.

St. Giles' Cathedral

Rutland St.

A700

St. John's

St. Cuthbert's

Edinburgh Castle

The Mound Pl.

Bank St.

Castlehill

Lawnmarket

Esplanade

National Library

Kings Stables Rd.

Johnston Terr.

Grassmarket

George IV Bridge

Castle Terr.

3

Greyfriars Kirk

Usher Hall

10

Lyceum

Kings Stables Rd.

Museum of Scotland

George Heriot's School

University of Edinburgh

Lauriston Pl.

TOLLCROSS

Glasgow

13

HILLHEAD

Great Western Rd.

A81

SPRINGBURN

A879

University of Glasgow

M8

Kelvingrove Park

14

COWCADDENS

15

N. Meadow Walk

George Sq. Lane

WEST END

Sauchiehall St.

12

11

TOWNHEAD

George St.

Clydeside Expwy.

CITY CENTRE

The Meadows

Clyde

BROOMIELAW

SALTMARKET

Glasgow Science Centre

GOVAN

Nelson St.

16

Gorbals St.

Glasgow Green

Paisley Rd.

M8

SOUTH SIDE

GORBALS

A700

Previous Page: Victoria Street, Edinburgh.

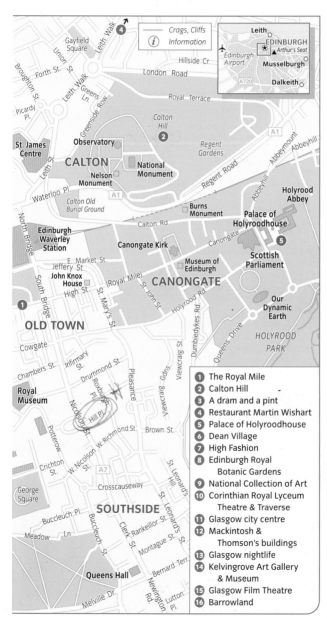

Crags, Cliffs
(i) Information

Leith
EDINBURGH
Arthur's Seat
Edinburgh
Airport
Musselburgh
A720
Dalkeith

Gayfield Square
Leith Walk
Hillside Cr.
London Road
Royal Terrace
Broughton St.
Forth St.
Union St.
Greens Ln.
Greenside Row
Picardy Pl.
Calton Hill
Regent Gardens
A1
Observatory
CALTON
Nelson Monument
National Monument
Abbeyhill
Abbeymount
Leith St.
St. James Centre
Waterloo Pl.
A1
Calton Old Burial Ground
Regent Road
Abbeyhill
Holyrood Abbey
North Bridge
Calton Rd.
Burns Monument
Palace of Holyroodhouse
Edinburgh Waverley Station
E. Market St.
Canongate Kirk
Canongate
Scottish Parliament
Jeffery St.
John Knox House
High St.
(Royal Mile)
St. Mary's St.
St. John St.
Museum of Edinburgh
CANONGATE
Holyrood Rd.
Dumbiedykes Rd.
Our Dynamic Earth
South Bridge
OLD TOWN
Cowgate
Queens Drive
HOLYROOD PARK
Chambers St.
Infirmary St.
Drummond St.
Roxburgh Pl.
Pleasance
Viewcraig St.
Viewcraig Gdns.
Royal Museum
Nicolson St.
Hill Pl.
W. Nicolson St.
W. Richmond St.
Brown St.
Potterow
Crichton St.
A7
Crosscauseway
St. Leonard's St.
St. Leonard's Hill
George Square
Buccleuch Pl.
SOUTHSIDE
Clerk St.
Rankeillor St.
Meadow Ln.
Buccleuch St.
Montague St.
Bernard Terr.
Queens Hall
Melville Dr.
Newington Rd.
Lutton Pl.

With the charm of its Old Town and castle, attractions ranging from national galleries to historic palaces, Edinburgh is one of Europe's foremost metropolises. Robert Louis Stevenson once said: 'No situation could be more commanding for the head city of a kingdom; none better chosen for noble prospects.' As you explore its sprawling gardens and majestic cathedrals, you'll be convinced what he wrote in the 19th century is no less true today. Across the country, Glasgow too offers some special moments.

❶ Take a stroll along the Royal Mile. The most famous boulevard in the city runs between the Castle and Palace, the historic road that traversed the most ancient part of Edinburgh, the UNESCO World Heritage Site of the Old Town. The best time to do this is at dusk, when the tourist crowds calm down. *See p 9.*

❷ Climb one of Edinburgh's hills. Bring your camera, of course, as the views can be breathtaking. Your most challenging option is Arthur's Seat in Holyrood Park. Stevenson's favorite vantage point was Calton Hill because he could see Edinburgh Castle, as well as Old and New Towns. You can cheat a bit by taking the lift to the top of the Museum of Scotland (p 10), which has a fine rooftop terrace. *See p 65-66.*

❸ Sample a dram and a pint. Edinburgh has many places to drop in for a whisky and glass of real ale. It can be one of the trendiest style bars in New Town, or a traditional pub just off the Royal Mile. As for brands, try a peaty Laphroig whisky from the Isle of Islay and a local beer, such as Deuchars (*dew*-kars) IPA. *See p 88.*

❹ Feast on haute cuisine. Edinburgh is now one of the best places in the UK to have a top-class meal. The leading ventures are Restaurant Martin Wishart, The Kitchin, and 21212 among others. All capitalize on quality local ingredients available, from hill lamb to sea loch langoustines (Dublin Bay prawns). *See Chapter 6.*

❺ Explore the Palace of Holyroodhouse. Among several historic attractions in Edinburgh, this one (the Windsors' home away from home) is arguably the best. The Palace underwent several periods of

Top class seafood at The Kitchin.

Dean Village.

construction, from the 15th to the 17th century. The adjacent ruins are of an abbey that was founded in 1128. *See p 25.*

⑥ Visit Dean Village. A *dean* (alternatively spelled dene) is a deep valley, and this one along the water of Leith has a historic Edinburgh settlement, where the largest of the city's grain mills were established, perhaps as early as the 12th century. Restored and conserved, the settlement is a charming retreat. *See p 69.*

⑦ Shop for high fashion. Between some homegrown boutique outfits in the West End, top labels at Harvey Nichols department store, classic styling at Jenners, vintage clothes in Stockbridge, or the aristocratic shops on New Town's George Street, Edinburgh is a plentiful source of retail therapy. *See Chapter 4.*

⑧ Get botanical at the Royal Gardens. This is one of the best, traditional parks in all of Great Britain. Begun as a center for studying the beneficial properties of plants, Edinburgh Royal Botanic Gardens now has acres of plush lawns, sweeping rock gardens, hundreds of flowering rhododendrons, and some impressive Victorian glasshouses with palms threatening to outgrow the towering spaces. *See p 15.*

⑨ Appreciate art in Edinburgh. The National Collection can be found in various galleries around the town. In the main buildings on Princes Street Gardens you can admire pieces ranging from Renaissance to Impressionist, as well as excellent examples of Scottish works, whether by the Glasgow Boys or Raeburn. Entry to all of the permanent holdings is free. *See p 27.*

⑩ See cutting edge dramatic performances. Be it a landmark production by the National Theatre of Scotland at the glorious Corinthian Royal Lyceum Theatre, an edgy dark comedy by one of Scotland's

Edinburgh Royal Botanic Garden.

Glasgow School of Art.

leading contemporary playwrights at the ground-breaking Traverse, or opera at the Festival Theatre, in season, theater offers many opportunities. *See Chapter 8.*

⓫ **Enjoy the energetic city centre of Glasgow.** While Edinburgh steals most of the headlines in traditional travel guides, tourists in the know recognize that the capital's rival, Glasgow, is the livelier of Scotland's dynamic duo: From the bustling shopping district of Buchanan Street to cultural corners across the town. *See Chapter 10.*

⓬ **See the greatness of buildings by Mackintosh & Thomson.** In the 19th century, Glasgow produced two of the greatest architects in Europe with Charles Rennie Mackintosh and Alexander 'Greek' Thomson. No trip to the city is complete without seeing an example or two of their works, especially the Glasgow School of Art and Holmwood House. *See p 130 and 131.*

⓭ **A night out on the town in Glasgow.** Glasgow is the nightlife mecca of the West Coast, with its combination of brasseries, bars, clubs, and live music venues, such as the King Tut's Wah Wah Hut and Mono which capitalize on the burgeoning band scene in the city. *See p 161.*

⓮ **Admire Glasgow's eclectic city art.** Between the Burrell Collection and the Kelvingrove Art Gallery and Museum, the Glasgow municipal art holdings are truly exceptional. *See p 119 and 121.*

⓯ **Catch some leading European cinema.** The **Glasgow Film Theatre** (GFT for short) offers an outstanding schedule of contemporary film, often from the continent, as well as the best of US independent and British art films. *See p 162.*

⓰ **Rock out one night in Glasgow.** The city's live music scene is quite legendary and deservingly so. Bands, whether touring megastars or local indie kids, get rousing receptions and respond in kind at venues like Barrowland or King Tut's Wah Wah Hut. *See p 164.* ●

The Best Full-Day Tours

The Best in **One Day**

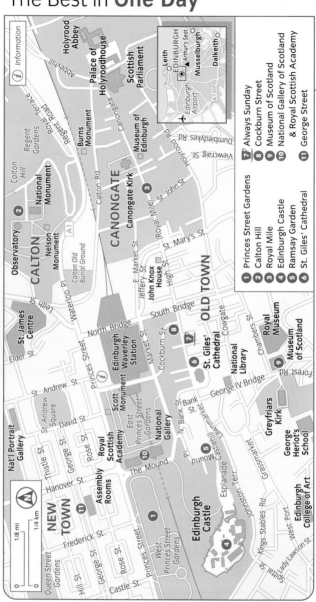

1 Princes Street Gardens
2 Calton Hill
3 Royal Mile
4 Edinburgh Castle
5 Ramsay Garden
6 St. Giles' Cathedral
7 Always Sunday
8 Cockburn Street
9 Museum of Scotland
10 National Gallery of Scotland & Royal Scottish Academy
11 George Street

Previous Page: Stained glass window, John Knox House.

With only 1 day to spend in Scotland's capital city, you will need to be quite selective about the places you visit. This tour concentrates primarily on the historic heart known as the Old Town (where the city first began)—though it will introduce you to some of the New Town, the largest UNESCO designated conservation area in Great Britain. START: **Princes St, at Waverley Bridge. Bus: 3, 10, 12, 17, 25, or 44.**

1 ★★ Princes Street Gardens. With Edinburgh Castle looming above, this is one of the most picturesque parks in Europe. As the steep banks indicate, this was once a body of water: In the early 19th century, a nasty sewage-filled loch, actually. How times have changed. Today, the 15-hectare (37-acre) oasis is a great spot for a picnic or you can join the locals and lounge on its grassy slopes on a nice day. ⏲ *45 min. Princes St. (at Waverley Bridge.)* ☎ *0131/529-4068. www.cac.org.uk. Admission free. Daily dawn–dusk.*

2 ★★★ Calton Hill. Rising 106m (348 ft.) over the city, this hill offers some of the best panoramic views of Edinburgh, and boasts two noteworthy memorials. The **National Monument**, an unfinished replica of the Parthenon that helped earn Edinburgh the name 'Athens of the North' honors those who died fighting in the Napoleonic Wars. The tower seen across the city is **Nelson Monument**, built in respect of the famous Admiral and rather aptly in the shape of an inverted telescope. US Civil War buffs should visit the **Lincoln Memorial** in the old Calton Burial Ground off Waterloo Place. ⏲ *1 hr. Waterloo Place, at the Royal High School. Tickets £3. Nelson Monument Apr–Sept Mon 1pm-6pm, Tue–Sat 10am-6pm; Oct–Mar Mon-Sat 10am-3pm. Bus: x25.*

3 ★★★ Royal Mile. This is the most famous street in Scotland; it runs for about 1.6km (1 mile) between Edinburgh Castle and the ancient **Palace of Holyroodhouse** (p 25), with plenty of attractions in between, such as the **John Knox House** (p 24). Walking is the best way to experience this truly ancient road, which follows the spine of one of Edinburgh's many hills. Be sure to explore some of the ancient, narrow alleys that jut off the Street: They reflect the cramped and slightly sinister feel of the medieval past with names such as **Flesh Market Close.** Note that the Royal Mile takes different names along its length (from west to east): Castlehill, Lawnmarket, High Street, and finally Canongate. ⏲ *1–2 hr. High St, at North Bridge. Bus: 28.*

4 Edinburgh Castle. I'm not completely sold on the focus of much of the castle's interior displays, centering as they do on military matters. Plus it is a pricey ticket. But for now, you should at least take a look at its ramparts and esplanade, located at the head of

Edinburgh Castle.

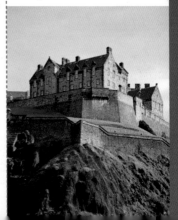

Ramsay Garden.

the Royal Mile. You'll get views in practically all directions, so have your camera ready. ⏱ *30 min. See p 23,* ❷.

❺ ★★ **Ramsay Garden.** While you're at the top end of the Royal Mile, I strongly encourage you to take time to admire these picturesque late 19th-century buildings named in honor of the poet Allan Ramsay (whose own home was once situated here). Perched on the southwestern ridge above Princes Street Gardens, this landmark is the brainchild of Sir Patrick Geddes (1854–1932). He was a city planner and general polymath whose efforts helped to conserve the Old Town you see today. Ramsay Garden is still used for private residences and, alas, visitors cannot explore inside. ⏱ *15 min. Castlehill (northeast corner of the castle esplanade). Bus: 28.*

❻ ★ **St. Giles' Cathedral.** For most of the Middle Ages, St. Giles was the only parish church in Edinburgh, which helps to explain both its size and location midway down the Old Town's main street. Originally constructed in the 12th century and named for the patron saint of cripples, the building survived English invaders who tried to burn it

down in 1385. Most of the current exterior of the church, also known as the High Kirk of St. Giles, is the result of Victorian renovations. On the sidewalk near the main entrance, make sure to note the heart-shaped arrangement of cobbles, which marks the site of the Old Tolbooth and a city jail—the latter referenced in Sir Walter Scott's history-filled novel *The Heart of Midlothian.* Spitting into it supposedly brings good luck. ⏱ *30 min. High St.* ☎ *0131/225-9442. www.stgiles cathedral.org.uk. Admission £3 donation suggested. May–Sept Mon–Fri 9am–7pm, Sat 9am–5pm, Sun 1–5pm; Oct–Apr Mon–Sat 9am–5pm, Sun 1–5pm. Bus: 35.*

❼ **Always Sunday** is a welcome break from the sometimes overly touristy competition on the Royal Mile. Come to this bright cafe for a wide-range of comforting homemade grub, such as butternut squash risotto, and cakes. *170 High St.* ☎ *0131/622-0667. www.always sunday.co.uk. Bus: 35. £.*

❽ **Cockburn Street.** This 'recent' addition to the Old Town cityscape was built in 1856 to make it easier to ascend the hill on which Old Town was built. Curvy Cockburn Street cuts across the original, extremely steep paths that descend precipitously down the hill from the Royal Mile toward Waverley train station. There is a mix of shops to browse in (CDs, clothing, art books, gifts), as well as some pubs and restaurants on this winding road. ⏱ *20 min. Between High St. and Market St. Bus: 35.*

❾ ★★ **Museum of Scotland.** This impressive sandstone structure contains exhibits outlining the story of Scotland, from its geology and ancient archaeology to late medieval royalty and 20th-century technology.

The Museum of Scotland.

On display are around 12,000 items, which range from 2.9-billion-year-old stones to a charming Hillman Imp, one of the last 500 automobiles manufactured in Scotland. The roof garden offers excellent views, while the recently upgraded **Royal Scottish Museum,** which has been incorporated into the modern building, includes a well-preserved and airy Victorian-era 'bird cage' main hall. ⏱ *2 hr. Chambers St.* ☎ *0131/247-4422. www.nms.ac.uk. Free admission. Daily 10am–5pm. Bus: 2, 7, 23, 31, 35, 41, or 42.*

⑩ ★★ National Gallery of Scotland & Royal Scottish Academy. Located on the Mound, a hump of earth that forms a land bridge between the Old and New Towns, this complex of Victorian exhibition halls is home to the National Galleries of Scotland's core collection of art. It includes Renaissance, Impressionist, and key Scottish pieces, including some by 'Glasgow Boy' James Guthrie. Thanks to the Weston Link, the National Gallery building, designed in 1850 by architect William Playfair (1790–1857), is tied internally to the Royal Scottish Academy building, also designed by Playfair in 1825.

The very modern halls (which include an excellent gift shop and good cafe with views of East Princes Street Gardens) provide a subterranean bridge between two outstanding examples of neoclassical architecture. ⏱ *30 min–2hr. The Mound.* ☎ *0131/624-6200. www. nationalgalleries.org. Free admission, except for temporary exhibits. Daily 10am–5pm (Thurs to 7pm). Bus: 3, 10, 12, 17, 25, 28, 41, or 44.*

⑪ ★★ George Street. A 1-day tour would not be complete without a visit to this broad boulevard at the core of Edinburgh's New Town. Devised during the reign of George III and constructed between 1766 and 1840, the New Town is now a UNESCO World Heritage Site. Notice how all the names of the main streets refer in some way to Hanoverian royalty, whether Frederick Street (George III's son) or Charlotte Street (George III's wife). Once the home of bankers, George Street is now one of the hottest shopping strips in Edinburgh, as well as the avenue with the city's trendiest bars, flashy restaurants, and dressy nightclubs. ⏱ *1 hr. George St., at Frederick St. Bus: 13, 24, 36, 41, or 42.*

The National Gallery of Scotland.

The Best in **Two Days**

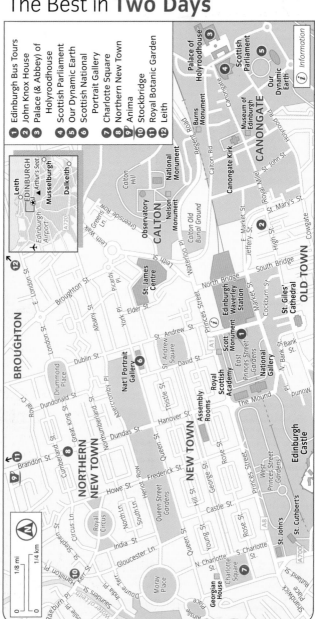

1 Edinburgh Bus Tours
2 John Knox House
3 Palace (& Abbey) of Holyroodhouse
4 Scottish Parliament
5 Our Dynamic Earth
6 Scottish National Portrait Gallery
7 Charlotte Square
8 Northern New Town
9 Anima
10 Stockbridge
11 Royal Botanic Garden
12 Leith

Over a couple of days you can dig a bit deeper and see nuances of Edinburgh, but I advise you to make an early start. With this tour you'll get a fuller picture of central Edinburgh, which is fairly compact. Use buses to get across Old Town and New Town, but when the weather is fine I suggest that you walk to many of the attractions on this tour and get a feel for the city. START: **Waverley Bridge. Bus: 10, 12, 17, 25, or 44.**

① ★★ Edinburgh Bus Tours. For entertaining and informative tours that offer an overview of the city's principal attractions, these open-top buses cannot be matched. During the trip you will see most of the major sights along the Royal Mile, and also get a gander at the Grassmarket, Princes Street, George Street, and more. The Majestic Tour buses—the ones that are blue and orange—don't take any longer, but deviate from the standard route— seeing fewer central Edinburgh landmarks but including the port of Leith. ⏱ 1½ hr. Waverley Bridge. ☎ 0131/220-0770. www.edinburgh tour.com. Tickets £12 adults, £11 seniors and students, £5 children, £28 family. Daily year-round every 15–20 min. 9:30am–5:30pm (till 7:30pm in summer).

② ★★★ John Knox House. This Royal Mile landmark (built in 1490) is difficult to miss, jutting out into the sidewalk on High Street with its cantilevered gable ends. There is some doubt that Scotland's most famous Reformation preacher, who was key to removing the Catholic Church as Scotland's official religious authority in the 16th century, actually lived here. The house is the real deal when it comes to photogenic 16th-century Edinburgh architecture. ⏱ 45 min. See p 24, **⑥**.

③ ★★ Palace (& Abbey) of Holyroodhouse. King David I established an abbey at the foot of the Royal Mile in 1128, with James IV (1473–1513) adding a palatial

residence in the 16th century. Although this early structure is mainly a ruin now, the palace was substantially altered in the 17th century to the state in which it currently stands. A critical episode in the fraught reign of Mary Queen of Scots (1542–87) was played out at Holyrood in 1566 when her loyal assistant David Rizzio was assassinated in the old north wing. The grounds include landscaped gardens and the **Queen's Gallery,** which exhibits a small part of the royal art collection. ⏱ 2 hr. See p 25, **⑧**.

④ ★ Scottish Parliament. After a right brouhaha over its cost (£500 million/nearly $1 billion at the time) and delays in construction, the new

King's Bed Chamber, Palace of Holyroodhouse.

The modern Scottish Parliament.

Scottish Parliament Building opened in the fall of 2004. Take the tour if you're really interested in Scottish government and want to see more of the modern interiors. Otherwise, it's a quick look and time to move on. ⏱ *10 min. (tour 1 hr). Holyrood Rd., across from the Queen's Gallery.* ☎ *0131/348-5000. www.scottish. parliament.uk. Free Admission. Tues–Thurs 9am–7pm (when Parliament is in session); Mon–Fri 9am–7pm (when Parliament is in recess); Apr–Oct 10am–6pm; Nov–Mar (and Sat–Sun year-round) 10am–4pm. Bus: 35.*

⑤ ★ kids Our Dynamic Earth. Under a tent-like canopy, this attraction celebrates the evolution and diversity of the planet, with an emphasis on seismic and biological activity. Simulated earthquakes, meteor showers, and views of outer space are part of the display. Skies in a tropical rainforest darken every 15 minutes, offering torrents of rain and creepy-crawlies underfoot. ⏱ *2 hr. See p 31,* ④.

⑥ ★ Scottish National Portrait Gallery. Part of the National Galleries of Scotland, this handsome red-stone neo-Gothic museum, designed by architect Sir Robert Rowand Anderson (1834–1921), houses many of the country's historic and current luminaries in portraiture from Mary Queen of Scots to the 21st-century composer James MacMillan, painted by everyone from Kokoschka to Raeburn. ⏱ *1 hr. See p 28,* ⑥.

⑦ ★ Charlotte Square. With a charming park at its core, this square, designed by the famous Georgian era designer Robert Adam, epitomizes the urbane grace of Edinburgh's New Town. You can almost imagine 18th-century horse-drawn carriages circumnavigating the place, with gaslights illuminating the sidewalks. You can tour the **Georgian House** on the north side of the square (see p 23). ⏱ *15 min. George St., at S. Charlotte St. Bus: 19, 36, or 41.*

⑧ ★ Northern New Town. Once Edinburgh's first New Town development was finished, work began north of Queen Street Gardens on a second model city. Architects William Sibbald (d. 1809) and Robert Reid (1775–1856) were the key designers in 1801, and used a grid pattern of streets, punctuated by "circuses" around arcs of handsome townhouses. At the northern edge of the development is Canonmills, so named for the milling community that served the abbey at Holyrood. ⏱ *30 min. Between Dublin St. and Royal Circus. Bus: 13, 24, 27, or 42.*

📻 **Anima** is the place to go for a decent Italian meal, or as they like to call it 'Italian soul food'. Choose from a widerange of pizzas, pastas, and both hot and cold sandwiches.

Despite its humble appearance, it also offers a fine wine list. *11 Henderson Row. ☎ 0131/558-2918. www.anima-online.co.uk. Bus: 23 or 27. £.*

⑩ ★★ **Stockbridge.** No matter how bustling Edinburgh gets during the tourist high season, this neighborhood just northwest of the city center seems to adopt a slower, calmer pace. Once a hippy enclave, and still possessing bohemian vibes, Stockbridge is currently one of the more affluent and desirable districts in which to live and play. Take time to stroll around the shops, and perhaps stopby a cafe or pub, such as the **Bailie Bar** (see p 88). 🕐 *45 min. Kerr St., at Hamilton Place. Bus: 24, 29, or 42.*

⑪ ★★★ **Royal Botanic Garden.** This is one of the grandest parks in the country, sprawling across some 28 hectares (69 acres). Edinburgh's first botanic garden was inaugurated in the late 17th century as a place for studying plants with medical uses. In spring, the various rhododendrons are almost reason alone to visit, but the plantings in all areas ensure year-round interest. 🕐 *1 hr. 20A Inverleith Row. ☎ 0131/552-7171. www. rbge.org.uk. Free admission (donations accepted). Daily Apr–Sept 10am–7pm; Mar and Oct–Dec 10am–6pm; Jan–Feb 10am–4pm. Bus: 8, 17, 23, or 27.*

⑫ ★ **Leith.** The Port of Leith is only a few kilometers north of the city center. The area is rapidly gentrifying, sadly losing some of its historic character as a rough-and-tumble maritime community. Still, you can use your imagination while wandering about the old docks near the street aptly named the Shore, which follows the Water of Leith as it spills into the harbor. One big attraction of the area is the pubs and restaurants, which include three with Michelin stars. 🕐 *1–2 hr. The Shore, at Bernard St. Bus: 7, 10, 16, 22, 35, or 36. Also see p 50.*

Inside a glasshouse at the Royal Botanic Garden.

The Best in **Three Days**

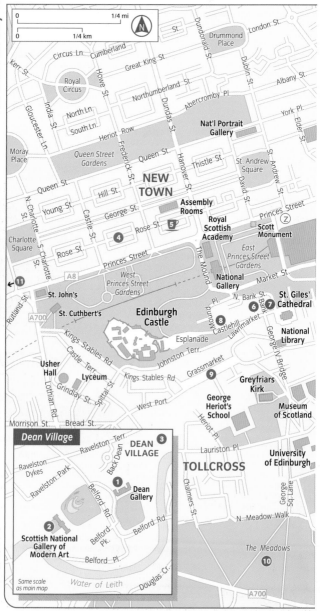

0	1/4 mi
0	1/4 km

N

Kerr St.

Circus Ln.   Cumberland

Drummond
Place

London St.

St.

Dundonald St.

Great King St.

Circus Ln.

Royal
Circus

Howe St.

Northumberland St.

Dublin St.

Albany St.

India St.

North Ln.

South Ln.

Abercromby Pl.

York Pl.

Gloucester Ln.

Heriot Row

Frederick St.

Dundas St.

Hanover St.

Nat'l Portrait
Gallery

Elder St.

Moray
Place

Queen Street
Gardens

Queen St.

Thistle St.

St. Andrew
Square

St. Andrew St.

Queen St.

Hill St.

**NEW
TOWN**

N. Charlotte St.

Young St.

Castle St.

George St.

Rose St.

Assembly
Rooms

Princes Street

David St.

Charlotte
Square

S. Charlotte St.

Rose St.

5

Royal
Scottish
Academy

Scott
Monument

Z

4

A8

Princes Street

East
Princes Street
Gardens

Market St.

11

West
Princes Street
Gardens

St. John's

National
Gallery

N. Bank St.

**St. Giles'
Cathedral**

Rutland St.

A700

St. Cuthbert's

**Edinburgh
Castle**

The Mound

Bank St.

6 **7**

Pl.

8

Castlehill
Lawnmarket

George IV Bridge

**National
Library**

Esplanade

Usher
Hall

Kings Stables Rd.

Castle Terr.

Johnston Terr.

Grassmarket

9

**Greyfriars
Kirk**

Lyceum

Grindlay St.

Spittal St.

Kings Stables Rd.

West Port

George
Heriot's
School

Heriot Pl.

**Museum
of Scotland**

Lothian Rd.

Morrison St.

Bread St.

Dean Village

Ravelston Terr.

Back Dean

3

**DEAN
VILLAGE**

Lauriston Pl.

TOLLCROSS

**University
of Edinburgh**

Ravelston
Dykes

Ravelston Park

1

Dean
Gallery

Chalmers St.

George Sq. Lane

2

Scottish National
Gallery of
Modern Art

Belford Rd.

Belford Pk.

Belford Rd.

N. Meadow Walk

*Same scale
as main map*

Belford Pl.

Water of Leith

Douglas Cr.

The Meadows

10

A700

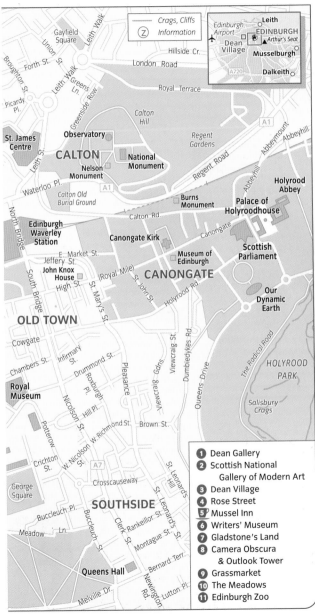

Crags, Cliffs
Ⓩ Information

Edinburgh Airport
Leith
EDINBURGH
Dean Village
Musselburgh
Arthur's Seat
Dalkeith
A720

Gayfield Square
Leith Walk
Union St.
Broughton St.
Forth St.
Picardy Pl.
Leith St.
St. James Centre
Waterloo Pl.
North Bridge
Leith Walk
Greenside Row
Greenside Ln.
Hillside Cr.
London Road
Royal Terrace
Calton Hill
Observatory
CALTON
Nelson Monument
National Monument
Calton Old Burial Ground
A1
Regent Gardens
Regent Road
A1
Abbeymount
Abbeyhill
Abbeyhill
Holyrood Abbey
Burns Monument
Calton Rd.
Palace of Holyroodhouse
Canongate
Edinburgh Waverley Station
E. Market St.
Jeffery St.
John Knox House
High St.
South Bridge
Canongate Kirk
Museum of Edinburgh
St. Mary's St.
(Royal Mile)
St. John St.
CANONGATE
Holyrood Rd.
Scottish Parliament
Our Dynamic Earth
OLD TOWN
Cowgate
Chambers St.
Infirmary St.
Royal Museum
Drummond St.
Roxburgh Pl.
Hill Pl.
Nicolson St.
Potterow
Crichton St.
George Square
W. Nicolson St.
W. Richmond St.
Pleasance
Brown St.
Viewcraig Gdns.
Viewcraig St.
Dumbiedykes Rd.
Queens Drive
The Radical Road
HOLYROOD PARK
Salisbury Crags
A7
Crosscauseway
SOUTHSIDE
Buccleuch Pl.
Meadow Ln.
Buccleuch St.
Clerk St.
Rankeillor St.
Montague St.
St. Leonard's Hill
St. Leonard's St.
Bernard Terr.
Queens Hall
Melville Dr.
Newington Rd.
Lutton Pl.

1 Dean Gallery
2 Scottish National Gallery of Modern Art
3 Dean Village
4 Rose Street
5 Mussel Inn
6 Writers' Museum
7 Gladstone's Land
8 Camera Obscura & Outlook Tower
9 Grassmarket
10 The Meadows
11 Edinburgh Zoo

Although you can see a lot over a few days, Edinburgh attractions—whether a branch of the National Gallery that highlights abstract art, one of the oldest houses on the Royal Mile, or a great museum for younger visitors—just keep on coming. With an extra day, you can traverse the city center from west to east and find some excellent spots to reflect on your time in the city. START: **Belford Rd., northwest of the city center. Bus: 13.**

1 ★ **Dean Gallery.** The most recent addition to the National Galleries of Scotland, the Dean is housed in the handsome former Dean Orphanage, admirable for its Tuscan style portico. The gallery often hosts touring, temporary exhibits of modern art and design, ranging from paintings by Picasso to plans and detailed drawings from architect Sir Basil Spence (1907–76). You will also find a permanent display of surrealist art and the re-created studio of pop artist Eduardo Paolozzi (1924–2005). ⏲ *1 hr. 73 Belford Rd.* ☎ *0131/624-6200. www. nationalgalleries.org. Free admission, except for some temporary exhibits. Daily 10am–5pm. Bus: 13 or National Galleries shuttle.*

2 ★ **Scottish National Gallery of Modern Art.** Across the road from the Dean, this branch of the Scottish National Galleries offers works by French post-impressionists Bonnard and Matisse; European expressionists, such as Kirchner and Nolde; and recent acquisitions from such contemporary Scottish artists as Christine Borland. All are housed in a neoclassical building that once functioned as John Watson's School—originally a refuge for children established in the 18th century by the wealthy solicitor. ⏲ *1 hr. See p 28,* **5**.

3 ★★ **Dean Village.** This enclave on the Water of Leith offers a break from the buzz of the bigger city. A milling village stood here probably

as early as the days of King David I in the 12th century. While nothing nearly that old survives today, Dean's attractive historic buildings were once in a terrible state until the middle of the 20th century, when conservation efforts helped to preserve their picturesque charm. ⏲ *30 min. Just west of the intersection of Queensferry and Belford Rds. Bus: 13 or 41. Also see p 69.*

4 ★ **Rose Street.** Rose Street was originally intended to provide homes and workshops for artisans in New Town, but today the road is probably best known for its pubs, which include the **Abbotsford** (p 88) with its Edwardian-era ceiling cornices and selection of fine real ales. ⏲ *1 hr. Between Princes St. and George St. Bus: 19, 23, 27, or 42.*

Modern Art at the Scottish National Gallery.

Rose Street is home to a host of shops, pubs and cafes.

Owned by shellfish farmers on Scotland's West Coast, the casual **5 Mussel Inn** serves great steaming bowls of fresh mussels and broth, grilled queen scallops, and other seafood options. Pots of mussels cost from £5 for half a kilo. *61–65 Rose St.* ☎ *0131/225-5979. www.mussel-inn.com. Bus: 19,23,27, or 42.* **££.**

6 ★ Writers' Museum. Devoted to Scotland's three paramount male authors—Burns, Scott, and Stevenson—this museum displays memorabilia in a notable 17th-century townhouse: Lady Stair House, built for Sir Walter Gray of Pittendrum in 1622 and conserved at the instigation of Sir Patrick Geddes (see also p 10, **5**) in 1893. My favorite museum items are the front-page London newspaper notice of Robert Burns' death in 1796 and the basement exhibit filled with various possessions of the great traveler Robert Louis Stevenson, including his riding boots and fishing rod. You can stock up on famous Scottish works in the small bookshop. ⏱ *1 hr. Lady Stair's Close, Lawnmarket.* ☎ *0131/ 529-4901. Free admission. Mon–Sat 10am–5pm; Sun (Aug only) noon–5pm. Bus: 28 or 41.*

7 ★★ Gladstone's Land. This is my favorite historic house in Edinburgh. The use of 'land' relates to the individual plot on which a building that faces the Royal Mile has been constructed. While quite narrow, the acreage of each land is usually deep, running down the hill away from the street. A merchant named Gladstone (then spelled Gladstane) took over this 16th-century property in 1617, adding on a new floor and also expanding the property toward the street. Architecturally exciting because much of the interior is unaltered, it has remnants of the colorfully decorated beams and lintels. Upstairs you can see the original external facade (now an interior wall) with friezes depicting classical columns and arches. ⏱ *45 min. 477B Lawnmarket.* ☎ *0131/226-5856. www.nts. org.uk. Admission £6 adults; £5 seniors, students and children, £15.50 family. Daily Apr–June, Sept–Oct 10am–5pm; July–Aug 10am–6:30pm. Bus: v23 or 41.*

Dimly-lit bedroom, Gladstone's Land.

The Meadows public park.

8 kids **Camera Obscura & Outlook Tower.** Putting a camera obscura here was the idea of Geddes, who worked tirelessly to prevent the wholesale demolition of Edinburgh's Old Town. Join one of the regular guided sessions for a birdseye view of the local surrounds. ⏲ *45 min. See p 31,* **1**.

9 ★ **Grassmarket.** In a city rich with history, the Grassmarket (both a street and plaza with a small city park in it) certainly has more than its share. Convicts were publicly hanged here until the 1780s, although the area was first intended as a weekly marketplace at the base of Castlehill. Robert Burns records staying at the Grassmarket's White Hart Inn. Indeed, today the area still has lots of pubs, hotels, and restaurants. ⏲ *45 min. Between West Port and West Bow. Bus: 2. See also p 45,* **13**.

10 ★★ **The Meadows.** This sprawling public park dating from the 1700s is a popular ground for sports ranging from golf to cricket. Tree-lined paths crisscross the playing fields and it's an excellent place for relaxing, or for the more energetic, playing Frisbee or kite flying. During the Edinburgh Festival big tents are erected here with loud live performances heard for miles around. ⏲ *1 hr. Melville Dr., at Lonsdale Terrace. Free admission. Daily dawn–dusk. Bus: 24 or 41.*

11 ★ kids **Edinburgh Zoo.** The premier animal attraction in Scotland, run by the Royal Zoological Society and focused on its role in wildlife conservation. ⏲ *2 hr. See p 32,* **6**. ●

Historic Edinburgh

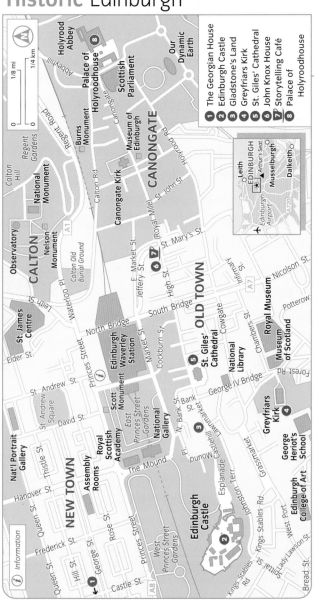

1 The Georgian House
2 Edinburgh Castle
3 Gladstone's Land
4 Greyfriars Kirk
5 St. Giles' Cathedral
6 John Knox House
7 Storytelling Café
8 Palace of Holyroodhouse

Previous Page: Palace of Holyroodhouse.

From Old Town to New Town, there is so much history to embrace in this city. The name of the Scottish capital probably stems from the Gaelic *Din Eidyn*, meaning 'fort on a hill slope'. The settlement of Edinburgh can be traced to the site of the city's castle, atop a sloping, rocky outcropping where a 6th-century hall is thought to have stood. START: **Charlotte Sq. Bus: 19, 36, or 41.**

Gladstone's Land.

❶ ★ The Georgian House. This historic townhouse displays the furnishings of a typical upper-class 18th-century Edinburgh household. Decor includes classic Chippendale chairs, a dining table set with fine Wedgwood china, and the piss pot that men apparently passed around for use at the dinner table, once their female companions had retired to different quarters. ⏱ *1 hr. 7 Charlotte Sq.* ☎ *0131/226-3318. www. nts.org.uk. Admission £6 adults; £5 seniors, students and children; £15.50 family. Daily July–Aug 10am–6pm; Apr–Jun, Sept–Oct 10am–5pm; Mar, Nov 11am–3pm.*

❷ Edinburgh Castle. Its earliest history is a bit vague, but in the 11th century, Malcolm III and his Saxon queen, later venerated as St. Margaret, founded a castle on this spot. In 1542, the castle ceased as a dedicated royal residence, having already begun to be used as an ordinance factory. The focus of the castle's exhibits today is weighted toward the military (the castle still barracks soldiers) and war history. Additionally, the **Great Hall** (where Scottish Parliaments used to convene) and the **Scottish Crown Jewels** are part of the self-guided tour. ⏱ *1¾ hr. to tour the interior. Castlehill.* ☎ *0131/225-9846. www. edinburghcastle.gov.uk. Admission £14 adults, £8.20 kids, £11.20 seniors and students. Daily Apr–Sept 9:30am–6pm; Oct–Mar 9:30am–5pm. Bus: 23 or 41.*

❸ ★★ Gladstone's Land. This 17th-century merchant's house gives a clear impression of the cozy living conditions some 400 years ago. The oldest part of the building is the rear wing, dating back to the 16th century. On the second level, a sensitively restored timber ceiling

Historic Greyfriars Kirk.

John Knox once preached at St. Giles' Cathedral.

looks suitably weathered and aged, but still bears colorful paintings of flowers and fruit. ⏱ *45 min. See p 19,* **7**.

4 ★ Greyfriars Kirk. Dedicated in 1620, this was the first 'reformed' church in Edinburgh, where the National Covenant, favoring Scottish Presbyterianism over the English Episcopacy, was signed in 1638 (an original copy remains here). Among many restorations of the kirk, one in the 1930s used California redwood to create the current ceiling. ⏱ *45 min. Greyfriars Place.* ☎ *0131/225-1900. www.greyfriarskirk.com. Free admission. Apr–Oct Mon–Fri*

10:30am–4:30pm, Sat 10:30am–2:30pm; Nov–Mar Thurs 1:30–3:30pm. Bus: 2, 23, 27, 41, 42, or 45. See also p 43, **2**.

5 ★ St. Giles' Cathedral. Its late medieval tower is a key city landmark, visible across central Edinburgh. Also called the High Kirk of St. Giles (which is the correct post-Reformation name), the building combines a dark and brooding Gothic stone exterior with surprisingly graceful buttresses. ⏱ *45 min. See p 10,* **6**.

6 ★★★ John Knox House. Knox (1510–72), the acknowledged

History in a Local Landmark

Across from the Canongate Kirk, and housed in part of historic Huntly House, is the **Museum of Edinburgh,** 142 Canongate (☎ 0131/529-4143; www.cac.org.uk). It concentrates on the capital's history and its traditional industries, such as glassmaking, pottery, wool processing, and cabinetry. One notable piece in the collection is the collar of **Greyfriars Bobby** (see p 43, **2**). Huntly House is actually three small 16th-century houses joined as one; it gets its name from a Duchess of the Gordons of Huntly who kept an apartment here in the 1700s. The museum is open Monday to Saturday from 10am to 5pm, and on Sunday (Aug only) from noon to 5pm. Admission is free.

father of the Presbyterian Church of Scotland, lived during a time of great religious and political upheaval. While some regard him as a prototypical Puritan, he actually proposed progressive changes and apparently had a sharp wit. Even if you're not interested in the firebrand reformer (who may have never lived here anyway), you should still visit this late 15th-century house, which is characteristic of the homes of this period. ◷ *45 min. 43–45 High St.* ☎ *0131/556-9579. www.scottishstorytelling centre.co.uk. Admission £4.25 adults, £3.75 seniors and students, £1 children. Daily July–Aug 10am–6pm; Sept–June Mon–Sat. Bus: 35.*

John Knox House, the former home of the father of the Scottish Reformation.

Next to John Knox House, in the Storytelling Centre, is the **7** **Storytelling Café**, run by the same good folk who run **Spoon** (see p 81). They serve a selection of sandwiches and soups until 6pm daily. *43–45 High St.* ☎ *0131/556-9579. www.scottishstorytellingcentre. co.uk. Bus: 35. £.*

Costume display at the Museum of Edinburgh.

8 ★★★ **Palace of Holyroodhouse.** The majority of the palace's current structure was built at the behest of King Charles II in the 1670s, although he ironically never stayed here. The current queen, however, does whenever she's in town, and you can see the reception rooms that she uses, such as the Throne Room. The real highlight of the tour is in the oldest surviving section of the palace (constructed around 1530), where Mary Queen of Scots resided. Be sure to check out some of the queen's needlework, which depicts her cousin (and the woman who had her beheaded), Elizabeth I, as a cat, and herself as a mouse. The audio tour is good, and the staff knowledgeable, so don't hesitate to ask questions. ◷ *1½ hr.* ☎ *0131/556-5100. www.royal.gov. uk. Admission £10.50 adults, £9.50 seniors and students, £6.35 children, £27.80 families. Daily Mar–Oct 9:30am–5pm; Nov–Feb 9:30am–3:30pm (closed when Royal Family in residence, 2 weeks in May–June). Bus: 35.*

Edinburgh for **Art Lovers**

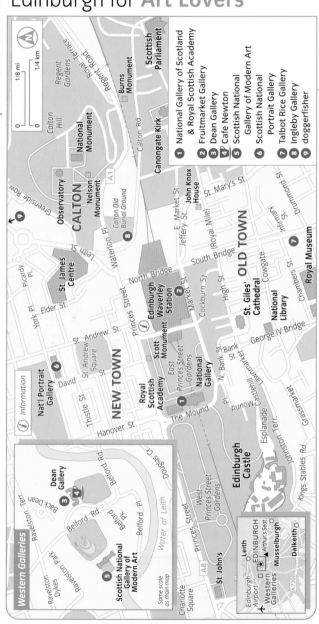

1. National Gallery of Scotland & Royal Scottish Academy
2. Fruitmarket Gallery
3. Dean Gallery
4. Cafe Newton
5. Scottish National Gallery of Modern Art
6. Scottish National Portrait Gallery
7. Talbot Rice Gallery
8. Ingleby Gallery
9. doggerfisher

Scottish Parliament

Regent Terrace

Royal Road

Regent Gardens

Burns Monument

Canongate Kirk

Calton Hill

National Monument

Nelson Monument

Observatory

CALTON

Calton Old Burial Ground

Calton Rd.

John Knox House

St. Mary's St.

E. Market St.

Jeffrey St.

South Bridge (Royal Mile)

St. Giles' Cathedral

OLD TOWN

Cowgate

Chambers St.

Royal Museum

Drummond St.

Infirmary St.

National Library

George IV Bridge

High St.

Cockburn St.

Market St.

North Bridge

Greenside Row

Leith St.

Waterloo Pl.

St. James Centre

Picardy Pl.

York Pl.

Elder St.

Princes Street

Edinburgh Waverley Station

Scott Monument

East Princes Street Gardens

Royal Scottish Academy

National Gallery

The Mound

St. Andrew St.

St. Andrew Square

Thistle St.

Hanover St.

David St.

Nat'l Portrait Gallery

i Information

NEW TOWN

Castlehill

Lawnmarket

Bank St.

N. Bank St.

St. Giles' St.

Esplanade

Johnston Terr.

Edinburgh Castle

West Princes Street Gardens

Princes Street

St. John's

Charlotte Square

Kings Stables Rd.

Grassmarket

Western Galleries

Dean Gallery

Scottish National Gallery of Modern Art

Back Dean

Belford Rd.

Belford Pl.

Ravelston Terr.

Ravelston Dykes

Ravelston Park

Douglas Cr.

Water of Leith

Belford Rd.

Some scale as main map

Edinburgh Airport

Leith

EDINBURGH

Arthur's Seat

Musselburgh

Western Galleries

Dalkeith

A720

A8

A1

0   1/8 mi
0   1/4 km

Edinburgh is home to some of the country's finest art, sculpture, and design. The National Gallery's classic master-pieces and the surrealist art of the Dean Gallery exist alongside the contemporary artworks found in smaller galleries scattered across the city. The result is an inspirational range of creativity, ranging from ancient to modern conceptual. START: **The Mound. Bus: 23, 27, 41, 42, or 45.**

① ★★ National Gallery of Scotland & Royal Scottish Academy. While the collection seems relatively small, these galler-ies only have room to show a lim-ited number of the country's total holdings, which include classics by Titian, El Greco, and Rembrandt. In the basement wing, Scottish art is highlighted. The pastoral scenes and square, chunky brushstrokes of the notable 19th-century 'Glasgow Boys', such as James Guthrie, are priceless. The gallery takes particu-lar pride in Sir Henry Raeburn's 1790s portrait, *The Reverend Robert Walker Skating on Duddingston Loch*. Next door to the National Gal-lery—and connected by the Weston Link—the RSA hosts major exhibi-tions, such as paintings by Monet or the late Joan Eardley. ⏱ *2 hr. See p 11,* ⑩.

② ★ Fruitmarket Gallery. The city's leading contemporary art gal-lery is housed in an old fruit market (built in 1938), which has been updated and modernized. It hosts exhibits of both local and interna-tionally renowned modern artists, from Yoko Ono to Nathan Coley. The bookshop and cafe are equally appealing. ⏱ *45 min. 45 Market St.* ☎ *0131/225-2383. www.fruitmarket. co.uk. Free admission. Mon–Sat 11am–6pm; Sun noon–5pm. Bus: 36.*

③ ★ Dean Gallery. Opened in 1999, the Dean Gallery is the perma-nent home for the Scottish National

Dean Gallery.

Galleries' Surrealist art, including works by Dali, Miró, and Picasso. The gallery hosts traveling and spe-cial exhibitions of 20th-century art. ⏱ *1 hr. See p 18,* ①.

④P Cafe Newton in the Dean Gal-lery offers a slightly more sophisti-cated dining experience than the usual museum cafes, with table ser-vice for hot dishes, cakes and cof-fee. *Dean Gallery, 73 Belford Rd.* ☎ *0131/624-6273. £.*

⑤ ★ Scottish National Gallery of Modern Art. Scotland's collection of late-19th and 20th-century art originally opened in 1960 in a building in the Royal Botanic Garden, until it moved to these premises in 1980. The collection is international in scope and quality, with works ranging from Matisse and Picasso to Balthus and Hockney. 🕐 *1 hr. 75 Belford Rd.* ☎ *0131/624-6200. www.nationalgalleries. org. Free admission, except for some temporary exhibits. Daily 10am–5pm. Bus: 13 or National Galleries shuttle.*

⑥ ★ Scottish National Portrait Gallery. Opened in 1889, the country's portrait gallery features many famous Scots, from Robert Burns to Sean Connery, as well as Enlightenment thinkers and some famous sports personalities too. The artists include Rodin, Ramsay, and Nasmyth. Highlights of the gallery's handsome central hall are the

The elaborate red brick facade of the National Portrait Gallery.

The Fruitmarket Gallery hosts shows by local and international artists.

ground-floor statues and the second-floor mural—and a 'pageant frieze'—that covers the walls with many noteworthy and historic Scottish folk, from St. Ninian to Adam Smith. The beautiful Venetian Gothic building was a gift to the country from the principal owner of the *Scotsman* newspaper, J. R. Findlay, who paid for its construction from 1885 to 1890. 🕐 *1½ hr. 1 Queen St.* ☎ *0131/624-6200. www.national galleries.org. Free admission, except for some temporary exhibits. Daily 10am–5pm. Bus: 4, 10, 12, 16, 26, or National Galleries shuttle.*

⑦ Talbot Rice Gallery. Part of the University of Edinburgh, and housed in the handsome Old College, the Talbot Rice displays the university's permanent art collection of Old Masters (in the William Playfair-designed Georgian Gallery) and puts on temporary shows by significant contemporary artists from around the world in the **White Gallery** and round room. The gallery is named after fine art professor David Talbot Rice, who taught at the university from 1934 to 1972. 🕐 *45 min. Old College, South*

National Galleries Bus

If you plan to visit the various branches of the Scottish National Galleries, from the Dean to the Portrait, a good way to get around is by using the free shuttle bus service that stops near or right at the entrances of them all. The buses run at 45-minute intervals from about 11am to 5pm daily, although you should check with gallery staff at each branch to confirm they're running on their regular schedule.

Bridge. ☎ 0131/650-2211. www.trg.ed.ac.uk. Free admission. Tues–Sat 10am–5pm. Bus: 3, 8, 29, or 49. Map p 26.

❽ Ingleby Gallery. The best independent gallery in Edinburgh, Ingleby represents a host of contemporary artists, whether Rachel Whiteread or Kenny Hunter. There's always something worthwhile to see here. ⏱ 45 min. 15 Calton Rd. ☎ 0131/556-4441. www.inglebygallery.com. Free admission. Mon–Sat 10am–5pm. Bus: 7, 14, 29, or 49.

❾ doggerfisher. If you prefer cutting edge, this gallery pushes the boundaries. You'll find installations, videos—and some paintings now and again. It's the one that London aesthetes look to for the latest in conceptual Scottish art. ⏱ 45 min. 11 Gayfield Sq. ☎ 0131/558-7110. www.doggerfisher.com. Free admission. Tues–Fri 11am–6pm; Sat noon–5pm, or by appointment. Bus: 10, 12, 14, or 22.

The doggerfisher gallery specializes in contemporary and conceptial Scottish art.

Edinburgh for Families

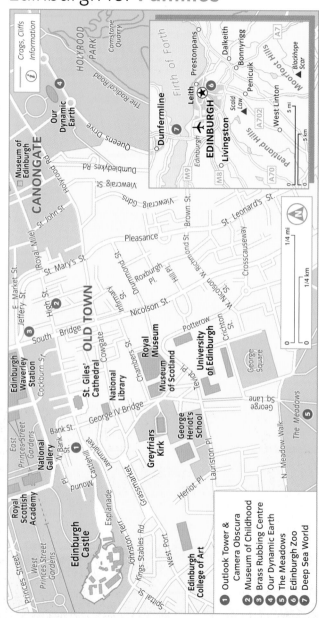

1 Outlook Tower &
  Camera Obscura
2 Museum of Childhood
3 Brass Rubbing Centre
4 Our Dynamic Earth
5 The Meadows
6 Edinburgh Zoo
7 Deep Sea World

Crags, Cliffs
(i) Information

Edinburgh has plenty of fun attractions for families—so if you tire of history and some of the more serious sites, check out my recommendations below. They include the hands-on exhibits at Our Dynamic Earth and a look at the toys that your great-great-grandparents may have once owned at the Museum of Childhood. Remember that for many of these exhibits, last admission is generally 1 hr. before closing. START: **Castlehill, Old Town.**

❶ Outlook Tower & Camera Obscura.
The 150-year-old periscope-like lens at the top of the Outlook Tower throws an image of nearby streets and buildings onto a circular table, and the moving 'picture' can be magically magnified with just a piece of cardboard. Guides reveal this trick, help to identify landmarks, and describe the highlights of Edinburgh's history. In addition, the observation deck offers free access to telescopes. *🕐 1 hr. Castlehill. ☎ 0131/226-3709. www.camera-obscura.co.uk. Admission £9.95 adults, £7.95 seniors and students, £6.95 children. Daily Apr–June 9:30am–6pm; July–Oct 9:30am–7:30pm; Nov–Mar 10am–5pm. Bus: 23, 27, 41, or 45.*

❷ ★ Museum of Childhood.
Allegedly the world's first museum devoted solely to the history of childhood, this popular and free museum is perhaps as much for the young at heart as for kids. The historic exhibits here range from valuable German Stieff teddy bears to an 18th-century Queen Anne doll and matchbox cars. *🕐 1 hr. 42 High St. ☎ 0131/529-4142. www.cac.org.uk. Free admission. Mon–Sat 10am–5pm, Sun noon–5 pm. Bus: 35.*

❸ ★ Brass Rubbing Centre.
Walk down Chalmers Close from the High Street to find the Brass Rubbing Centre, located in the remnants of the Holy Trinity church, founded in the 1460s. At this lesser-known and calm attraction, visitors make wax rubbings or impressions from all sorts of designs, whether prehistoric motifs or Celtic crosses. Costs start from about £2 for simple rubbings that might take up to an hour to execute. *🕐 1 hr. Chalmers*

A polar region simulation at Our Dynamic Earth.

The Camera Obscura offers a 360-degree view of the city.

Close. ☎ 0131/556-4364. www.cac. org.uk. Free admission. Apr–Sept Mon–Sat 10am–5pm (also Sun noon–5pm in Aug); closed Nov–Mar. Bus: 36.

④ ★ **Our Dynamic Earth.** Under a tent-like canopy near the New Scottish Parliament, Our Dynamic Earth celebrates the evolution and diversity of the planet, with emphasis on the seismological and biological processes that led from the Big Bang to the world we know today. There is the slimy green primordial soup where life began and a series of specialized aquariums, some with replicas of early life forms, and a simulated tropical rainforest where skies darken at 15-minute intervals, offering torrents of rainfall and creepy-crawlies underfoot. You will also find a restaurant, cafe, play area, and a gift shop. ⏱ 2 hr. Holyrood Rd. ☎ 0131/550-7800. www.dynamic earth.co.uk. Admission £11.90 adults, £10.50 seniors and students, £7.95 children, 3–15 years. Apr–Oct daily 10am–5:30pm; Nov–Mar Wed–Sun 10am–5:30pm. Bus: 35 or 36.

⑤ ★★ **The Meadows.** Need some open space? This expansive public park has plenty of relaxing and picnicking potential amid the tree-lined paths and playing fields. ⏱ 1 hr. See p 20, ⑩.

⑥ ★ **Edinburgh Zoo.** Scotland's largest animal collection is 4½ km (3 miles) west of Edinburgh's city center on 32 hectares (80 acres) of hillside parkland. The zoo contains more than 1,500 animals, including white rhinos, pygmy hippos, and others. It also boasts the largest penguin colony in Europe housed in one of the world's biggest enclosures. From April to September, a penguin parade is

Deep Sea World

held daily at 2:15pm. ⏱ *2 hr. 134 Corstorphine Rd.* ☎ *0131/334-9171. www.edinburghzoo.org.uk. Admission £15.50 adults, £ 13 seniors and students; £11 children, £47.70 families. Daily Apr–Sept 9am–6pm; Oct and Mar 9am–5pm; Nov–Feb 9am–4:30pm. Bus: 12, 26, 31, or 100 (Airlink).*

❼ **Deep Sea World.** In the early 1990s, a group of entrepreneurs sealed the edges of an abandoned rock quarry under the Forth Rail Bridge near North Queens Ferry, filled it with sea water, and positioned a 112m (370-ft.) acrylic tunnel on the bottom. Stocked with a menagerie of sea creatures, this section of artificial ocean is Scotland's most comprehensive aquarium. From the submerged tunnel you view kelp forests; sandy flats favored by bottom-dwelling schools of stingray, turbot, and sole; and murky caves that shelter conger eels and small sharks. Curiously, the curvature of the tunnel's thick clear plastic makes everything seem about 30% smaller than it really is. For £75 each, kids can take a 'bubblemaker' dive with qualified scuba instructors. ⏱ *2 hr. Battery Quarry, North Queensferry (20 min. from Edinburgh).* ☎ *01383/411-880. www.deepseaworld.com. Admission £12 adults, £ 10.50 seniors and students, £8.25 children, £40 family. Daily 10am–6pm. Train: North Queens Ferry.*

Family Festivals

The festival programme that runs throughout the year in Edinburgh has plenty going on to get families involved, and it's not just the Summer months that are exciting either. In April, the city is host to the annual **International Science Festival** (www.sciencefestival.co.uk), an event featuring numerous workshops from multi-shape bubble blowing to robotics adventures, and for older teenagers (14+) discussions on genetics. The following month, in May, the **Scotland Imaginate Festival** (www.imaginate.org.uk) opens up the performing arts with a diverse programme featuring, for example, dramatic adaptations of Phillip Pullman stories, puppet theater shows and Shakespeare. Come the Summer months and August is the busiest time to visit with several events happening at once: catch a play during the fringe, or one of the hundred plus events aimed at younger visitors at the **Edinburgh International Book Festival** (www.edbookfest.co.uk), where parents can even learn how to read better bedtime stories, if their skills need some polishing. September brings the colorful **Mela** weekend (www.edinburgh-mela.co.uk), where families have their own area (from noon-6pm), although there is plenty going-on elsewhere, from lively dance acts to fashion shows, so teenagers won't be bored either. During October, visitors can join in the **Scottish International Storytelling Festival** (www.scottishstorytellingcentre.co.uk), attracting tale-tellers with both traditional and modern yarns about life, culture and travel. For comprehensive information on Edinburgh festivals, look at **www.edinburghfestivals.co.uk.**

Literary Edinburgh

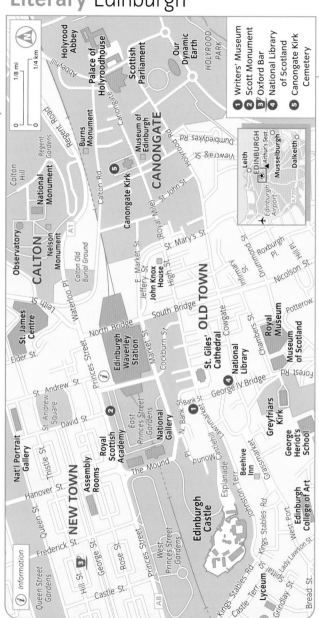

1 Writers' Museum
2 Scott Monument
3 Oxford Bar
4 National Library of Scotland
5 Canongate Kirk Cemetery

Holyrood Abbey
Palace of Holyroodhouse
Scottish Parliament
Our Dynamic Earth
HOLYROOD PARK

Abbeyhill
Regent Road
Burns Monument
Museum of Edinburgh
Canongate

Regent Gardens
Calton Hill
National Monument
CALTON
Observatory
Nelson Monument
Calton Old Burial Ground

Leith St.
Waterloo Pl.
St. James Centre
Elder St.

Nat'l Portrait Gallery
NEW TOWN
Assembly Rooms
Royal Scottish Academy

Queen Street Gardens
Hill St.
Hanover St.
Queen St.
Thistle St.
George St.
Rose St.
Frederick St.
Castle St.
Princes Street
West Princes Street Gardens

Edinburgh Castle

St. Andrew St.
St. Andrew Square
David St.

The Mound
East Princes Street Gardens
National Gallery

Princes Street
Edinburgh Waverley Station

North Bridge
South Bridge
Market St.
Cockburn St.

John Knox House
High St.
E. Market St.
Jeffery St.
St. Mary's St.

(Royal Mile)
St. John St.
Canongate
CANONGATE

Holyrood Rd.
Viewcraig St.
Dumbiedykes Rd.

Calton Rd.
Canongate Kirk

St. Giles' Cathedral
OLD TOWN
National Library
George IV Bridge
Cowgate
Chambers St.

Bank St.
N. Bank St.
Lawnmarket
Castlehill
Mound Pl.
Beehive Inn
Grassmarket
Esplanade
Johnston Terr.
West Port
Castle Terr.
King's Stables Rd.
Kings Stables Rd.

Greyfriars Kirk
George Heriot's School
Edinburgh College of Art
Royal Museum
Museum of Scotland
Forrest Rd.

Potterow
Nicolson St.
Infirmary St.
Drummond St.
Roxburgh Pl.

Lyceum
Spittal St.
Lady Lawson St.
Grindlay St.
Bread St.

A8
Information
ⓘ Information

Leith
EDINBURGH
Arthur's Seat
Musselburgh
Dalkeith
Edinburgh Airport
A720

0   1/8 mi
0   1/4 km

From, Walter Scott, the virtual inventor of the historic novel in the 1800s, to Ian Rankin, today's master of crime mysteries, Edinburgh has spawned and inspired many a great writer. In recognition, it recently became UNESCO's first International City of Literature (www.cityofliterature.com). START: **The Royal Mile, Lady Stair's Close. Bus: 23 or 41.**

The Writers' Museum salutes many of Scotland's best-known scribes.

1 ★ Writers' Museum. This 17th-century house contains a treasure-trove of portraits, relics, and manuscripts relating to Scotland's greatest men of letters: Robert Burns (1759–96), Sir Walter Scott (1771–1832), and Robert Louis Stevenson (1850–94). The museum building, Lady Stair's House, with its narrow passages and low clearances, was originally built in 1622. ⏱ 1 hr. See p 19, **6**.

2 Scott Monument. In the center of this 60-plus-meter (200-ft.) tower's Gothic spire is a marble statue of Sir Walter Scott and his dog, Maida, with Scott's fictional heroes carved as small figures in many niches throughout the steeple-like structure. Climb the 287 stairs to the top for worthwhile views. Look east and you can clearly see the Burns Monument, designed by Thomas Hamilton in 1830, on the side of Calton Hill. ⏱ 45 min. See p 49, **11**.

3 ★ Oxford Bar. This unassuming pub is the occasional hangout of leading crime author Ian Rankin—and it was the regular dive for his most famous character, the world-weary Inspector Rebus. A great place for a pint, but squeeze past the people at the small bar and into a side room, where there's more space and usually a gas fire burning. Food is limited to snacks. 8 Young St. ☎ 0131/539-7119. www.oxford bar.com. Bus: 13, 19, or 41. £.

The statue of Sir Walter Scott, part of the Scott Monument.

4 National Library of Scotland. Formed in 1925, the country's central library hosts readings and activities throughout the year, plus summer exhibitions. Apparently each and every book published in the UK and Ireland is on the shelves here; one of its most important holdings is a complete copy of the Gutenberg Bible (1455). ⏱ *1 hr. George IV Bridge.* ☎ *0131/623-3700. www.nls.uk. Free admission. Exhibitions June–Oct Mon–Sat 10am–5pm, Sun 2–5pm. Bus: 2, 23, 27, 41, 42, or 45.*

5 ★ Canongate Kirk Cemetery. Several literary connections are found here, from the grave of Adam Smith, who wrote *The Wealth of Nations,* to that of Robert Burns' paramour Agnes McLehose (his beloved Clarinda). Burns also arranged for the kirkyard's 1789 monument to poet Robert Fergusson, which bears an inscription by Burns: 'This simple Stone directs Pale Scotia's way/To pour her

A grave at the historic Canongate Kirk Cemetery.

sorrows o'er her Poet's dust.' ⏱ *1 hr. Canongate, the Royal Mile. Free admission. Daily dawn–dusk. Bus: 35.* ●

Following in Authors' Footsteps

The Literary Pub Tour retraces the footsteps of Burns, Stevenson, and Scott via the city's more atmospheric taverns, highlighting the tales of *Jekyll and Hyde* or the erotic love poetry of Burns. The walking tour costs £7 and departs nightly at 7:30pm (June–Sept) from the **Beehive Inn** on the Grassmarket (☎ 0131/226-6665; www.edinburghliterarypubtour.co.uk).

Complete with readings and dramatizations, the **Edinburgh Book Lovers' Tour** (☎ 01573/223-888; www.edinburghbookloverstour.com) departs from the **Writers' Museum** (see 1). Its guide is Allan Foster, the author of *The Literary Traveler in Edinburgh*, a compendium of writers' observations and quips about their stays and visits to Edinburgh. Described as an odyssey around Old Town, this walking tour costs £10 and departs at 10:30am and 1:30pm Saturday and Sunday throughout the year, and daily during the Edinburgh Festival.

The **Royal Mile**

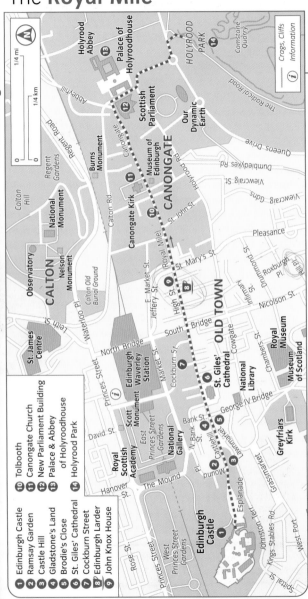

1 Edinburgh Castle
2 Ramsay Garden
3 Castle Hill
4 Gladstone's Land
5 Brodie's Close
6 St. Giles' Cathedral
7 Cockburn Street
8 Edinburgh Larder
9 John Knox House
10 Tolbooth
11 Canongate Church
12 New Parliament Building
13 Palace & Abbey of Holyroodhouse
14 Holyrood Park

Previous Page: New Scottish Parliament.

Situated on a mile-long ridge, Old Town is for many visitors the most historically and architecturally evocative district in Edinburgh. In the most part, the city's current reputation for beauty and romance rests upon the appearance of the Royal Mile, which runs along the spine, and its surrounding streets. START: **the esplanade of Edinburgh Castle.**

1 Edinburgh Castle. The esplanade of Edinburgh Castle has the most accessible views of the city in practically all directions. Evidence of buildings on the castle site dates from the 11th century, although fortifications of some kind on this mount, known as Castle Rock, may go back as far as the 6th century. *See p 23, 2.*

2 ★★ Ramsay Garden. Not a garden but an innovative and charming set of buildings that was the brainchild of Sir Patrick Geddes. The architecture is a beautiful mix of Scottish baronial and English cottage, combining corbels (the cantilevered round extensions), conical roofs, crow steps, and a half-timber gable construction. A polymath and city planner, Geddes almost single-handedly revived the fortunes of Old Town, working to rid it of squalid living conditions while saving it from total destruction and redevelopment. *See p 10, 5.*

3 ★ Castle Hill. The Royal Mile is formed by a series of roads that run from the castle to the palace at the east. The first short section is Castle Hill, followed by the Lawnmarket, High Street, and Canongate. On the right as you walk down the road are Cannonball House and Boswell's Court, which was originally built around 1600 and is now the site of a plush restaurant called the **Witchery** (p 82). Across the street is Geddes' observatory, which houses his **Camera Obscura** (p 31, 1), for unique views of the city.

4 ★★ Gladstone's Land. Between the 14th and 15th centuries, the plots (or tofts) on the Royal Mile were subdivided into forelands and backlands. Just past the entrances to James Court is Gladstone's Land, which dates to at least the 16th century and was purchased by Thomas Gladstone (then spelled Gladstane) in 1617. Nearby, **Lady Stair's Close** has the early-17th-century Lady Stair's House, the remnants of which now contain the Writers' Museum (p 19, 6) with exhibits dedicated to Burns, Scott, and Stevenson. *See p 19, 7.*

5 Brodie's Close. A site associated with one of Edinburgh's darker stories. The city has witnessed its fair share of infamous characters, and one fine example is the craftsman William Brodie: Upstanding gentleman and deacon of trades by day, but thief and ne'er-do-well by night. In 1788 he was hanged, ironically, on gallows of his own design. Robert Louis Stevenson is said to have had a childhood nightmare about the two-faced Brodie, which later became inspiration for his character Dr. Jekyll and Mr. Hyde. Lest you worry about the morality of Edinburgh, the close is actually named after Brodie's father, Francis, a gifted, law-abiding cabinetmaker. *304 Lawnmarket.*

6 ★ St. Giles' Cathedral. You're now on High Street. There is nearly as much history around St. Giles, or the High Church, as the city itself. Its origins date to the 12th

St. Giles' Cathedral on High Street.

century and it has been rebuilt and renovated repeatedly. All that really remains of the 15th-century church is the spire, a familiar landmark of the city. In the sidewalk near the Royal Mile, note the heart-shaped arrangement of cobbles. This marks the site of a city prison, made famous by Sir Walter Scott's *The Heart of Midlothian*. Spitting in the heart is said to bring good luck. Nearby in the Anchor Close, the first edition of the Encyclopaedia Britannica was printed. *See p 10,* **6**.

7 Cockburn Street. This curving street, heading down the hill to the north, is a relatively recent addition, built in 1856 to improve access to Waverley railway station. The road traverses the old closes and stairs (such as the Fleshmarket Close) that descend steeply down the hill from the Royal Mile.

The cozy **8 Edinburgh Larder** is located just a few paces off the Royal Mile. Soups, sandwiches, and house specials such as sausage

hotpot or goat's cheese frittata are served daily. *15 Blackfriars St.,* ☎ *0131/556-6922. www.edinburgh larder.co.uk. £.*

9 ★★★ John Knox House. Jutting out into the wide sidewalk of High Street is this photogenic and apparently genuine 16th-century house. Although any real link to Knox (the firebrand Protestant reformer), has been debated over the years, at least the perceived connection did ensure that this remarkable building was preserved. Next door is **Moubray House,** which has some of the same late medieval details of Gladstone's Land (**4**). The rear portion (unfortunately not open to the public) might actually date to 1530, making it perhaps the oldest surviving dwelling in the city. *See p 24,* **6**.

10 ★★ Tolbooth. The tower of the Tolbooth was built around 1590 and the attractive clock that extends out over the street was added to the building in the 1880s. Inside you can find the museum called **People's Story.** You are now on the portion of the Royal Mile known as the Canongate. Here, outside the town's earliest protective walls, the original settlement of Canongate was only formally incorporated into the city of Edinburgh in 1856.

⓫ ★ **Canongate Church.** The original parish church for the Canongate burgh was Holyrood Abbey (⓭), but eventually a new kirk became necessary, and so this site, with its bell-shaped roofline, was christened in 1691. The churchyard has good views of the **Royal High School** on Calton Hill, and is the home of several gravestones of notable folk including pioneer economist Adam Smith, Robert Burns' lover Clarinda, and allegedly the personal assistant of Mary Queen of Scots, Rizzio. *153 Canongate.*

⓬ ★★ **New Parliament Building.** Subject to seemingly endless debate, the construction of the new Parliament Building for Scotland, (designed by Enric Miralles, a Barcelona-based architect), was finally started. Whatever the controversy, the city has one of the most intriguing governmental buildings built in the last 100 years. The abstract motif, repeated on the facade along the Canongate, was apparently inspired by Raeburn's painting of *Reverend Robert Walker Skating on Duddingston Loch,* which hangs in the Scottish wing of the National Gallery of Art on the Mound (see p 11, ⓾).

⓭ ★★★ **Palace & Abbey of Holyroodhouse.** The abbey (now in ruins) on the grounds of Holyroodhouse dates to the reign of King David I (in the early 12th century). Much further into the royal lineage, James IV expanded the buildings, as did his heir—all to be renovated yet again in the 17th century by King Charles II, who apparently never even visited the palace. Only after the first visit by Queen Victoria in the 1840s have its lodgings been regularly used by members of the Royal Family. *See p 25,* ⑧.

⓮ ★★ **Holyrood Park.** If you have any energy left, the 160-plus hectares (400 acres) of Holyrood Park allow plenty of ground to roam. From here you can scale **Salisbury Crags** and mount the high hill known as **Arthur's Seat** (see p 64-67), which rises some 251m (825 ft.) above Edinburgh. Nearby is the science and family-oriented tourist attraction, **Our Dynamic Earth** (p 31, ④).

John Knox House dates back to the 16th-century.

THE PREACHER

JOHN KNOX IS ABLE IN ONE HOUR TO PUT MORE LIFE IN US THAN FIVE HUNDRED TRUMPETS CONTINUALLY BLASTING IN OUR EAR

The Best Neighborhood Walks

The **Southside**

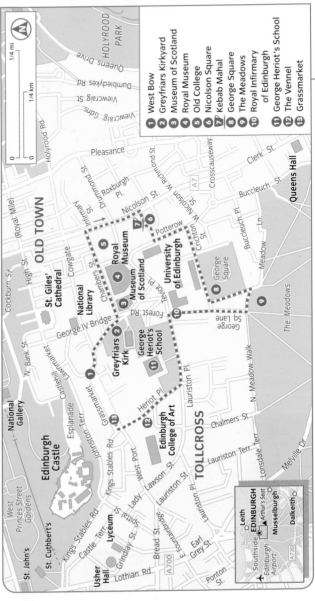

1 West Bow
2 Greyfriars Kirkyard
3 Museum of Scotland
4 Royal Museum
5 Old College
6 Nicolson Square
7 Kebab Mahal
8 George Square
9 The Meadows
10 Royal Infirmary of Edinburgh
11 George Heriot's School
12 The Vennel
13 Grassmarket

1/4 mi

1/4 km

HOLYROOD PARK

Queens Drive

Dumbiedykes Rd.

Viewcraig St.

Viewcraig Gdns.

Holyrood Rd.

Pleasance

Royal Mile

OLD TOWN

Cowgate

High St.

Royal Mile

Cockburn St.

St. Giles' Cathedral

National Library

George IV Bridge

Chambers St.

Infirmary St.

Drummond St.

Roxburgh Pl.

Nicolson St.

Potterow

Crosscauseway

A7

S. Nicolson St.

W. Richmond St.

Crichton St.

George Square

Buccleuch St.

Clerk St.

Queens Hall

Buccleuch Pl.

Meadow Ln.

University of Edinburgh

Forrest Rd.

Teviot Pl.

George Sq. Lane

The Meadows

N. Bank St.

Castlehill

Lawnmarket

Greyfriars Kirk

George Heriot's School

Heriot Pl.

Lauriston Pl.

N. Meadow Walk

Royal Museum

Museum of Scotland

Castlehill

Esplanade

Johnston Terr.

Grassmarket

Edinburgh College of Art

Lauriston St.

Lauriston Pl.

Chalmers St.

TOLLCROSS

Edinburgh Castle

National Gallery

West Princes Street Gardens

St. Cuthbert's

St. John's

Usher Hall

Lyceum

Kings Stables Rd.

Castle Terr.

Spittal St.

Grindlay St.

Lothian Rd.

West Port

Lady Lawson St.

Bread St.

Fountainbridge

Earl Grey St.

Ponton St.

Lauriston Terr.

Lonsdale Terr.

Melville Dr.

Kings Stables Rd.

A700

A700

Leith

EDINBURGH

Arthur's Seat

Musselburgh

Southside

Edinburgh Airport

A720

Dalkeith

This walk combines parts of Old Town with the historic settlements south of the original burgh, an area now dominated by the University. The fortifications that once surrounded the medieval city, such as the Flodden Wall, were generally expanded each time they needed improving, eventually encompassing the districts of Grassmarket and ancient streets such as the Cowgate.

START: **West Bow and the Grassmarket.**

❶ ★ West Bow. Originally this street zigzagged up the steep slope from the Grassmarket to Castlehill. Combined with Victoria Street (added in the 19th century), it now forms a charming arc to the Royal Mile via the **George IV Bridge,** and is filled with unpretentious shops, bars, and restaurants. At the base of the street is **West Bow Well,** which was built in 1674. *East end of the Grassmarket.*

❷ ★★ Greyfriars Kirkyard. Completed in 1620, the church (see p 24, ❹) was built amid a cemetery (or kirkyard) that Queen Mary proposed in 1562 because burial space at **St. Giles' Cathedral** (p 10, ❻) was exhausted. The kirkyard contains a section of the **Flodden Wall,** built after the Scots' disastrous

Farming display in the Museum of Scotland.

The statue of Greyfriars Bobby, the faithful policeman's dog.

defeat at Flodden in the early 16th century. Amid many 17th-century monuments, the cemetery's most celebrated grave is that of a 19th-century policeman whose faithful dog, Bobby, reputedly stood watch over the plot for 14 years. Greyfriar Bobby's statue is at the top of Candlemaker Row, just outside the pub named in his honor. *Candlemaker Row, at Chambers St.* ☎ *0131/225-1900. www.greyfriars kirk.com.*

❸ ★★ Museum of Scotland. This striking contemporary edifice was designed by architects Benson and Forsyth and built mostly of beige sandstone from the northeast of Scotland. Opened in the late 1990s, it was purpose-built for exhibitions that chart the history of Scotland. *See p 10, ❾.*

The Royal Museum.

Along the north side of the square, **7** **Kebab Mahal** serves up inexpensive but tasty and generous portions of Indian food. Although takeaways include kebabs and pizza, the Indian specialties cover most popular curries. Its down-to-earth atmosphere draws a cross-section of diners, from professors and students to visitors of the nearby central mosque. *7 Nicolson Sq.* ☎ *0131/622-5214. www.kebab-mahal.co.uk. £.*

4 **Royal Museum.** This Victorian-era museum is one of the architectural highlights on Chambers Street, a broad but short boulevard named after a 19th-century lord provost (the equivalent of a mayor). The museum was designed by the same architects responsible for London's Royal Albert Hall. *Chamber St.*

5 ★★ **Old College.** The 1781 exteriors of the University of Edinburgh Old College have been called the greatest public work by neoclassical architect Robert Adam (1728–92). This 'Old College' actually replaced an earlier version of the same name, dating to the 1500s. Construction of the quadrangle of buildings was suspended during the Napoleonic wars, and William Playfair designed the Quad's interiors in 1819. *Chambers St, at South Bridge. www.ed.ac.uk.*

6 **Nicolson Square.** This small plaza dates to 1756, and the buildings along its north fringe were apparently the first to be built in this area. In the square's park is the **Brassfounders' Column,** designed in 1886 for the International Exhibition in Edinburgh by esteemed architect and city planner Sir James Gowans (1822–90).

8 ★ **George Square.** Almost entirely redeveloped (and architecturally ruined) by the University of Edinburgh in the 20th century, George Square was originally complete with uniform mid-18th-century townhouses—a few of which still remain on the west end. You may also assume that the square was named in honor of a king, but it actually bears the first name of the brother of the designer, James Brown. *Crichton St, at Charles St.*

9 ★★ **The Meadows.** This large public park was once a loch (the South Loch, to be exact), but it was

George Heriot's School.

Weekly markets were held in the Grassmarket for nearly 400 years, but today people flock here for the pubs and cafes.

filled and today is a large green expanse crisscrossed by tree-lined paths. At the western end of the park is **Bruntsfield Links,** which some speculate entertained golfers in the 17th century and still has a multi-hole pitch-and-putt course. *Golf can be played May–Sept, dawn–dusk for free. No rental clubs or balls. See also p 20,* ⑩.

⑩ **Royal Infirmary of Edinburgh.** The expansive grounds of the Royal Infirmary of Edinburgh include George Watson's Hospital, which dates to the 1740s. Wards in the grand Victorian-era baronial buildings were among the first to incorporate the open-plan layouts of Florence Nightingale, who approved the designs. To the east is the University of Edinburgh's Medical School. It faces **Teviot Place,** a hot-bed of university life, filled with popular cafes and bars, seemingly open and bustling at all hours of the day and night. *Forrest Rd, at Bristo Place.*

⑪ **George Heriot's School.** Heriot (1563–1624) was nicknamed the 'Jinglin' Geordie'. As jeweler to King James VI, he exemplified the royal entourage who left the country when James became king of England as well as Scotland. Although

Heriot went on to make his fortune in London, he did bequeath several thousand pounds to build this facility (now a private school) for Edinburgh's disadvantaged boys, which opened in 1659. Of the 200-odd windows in the Renaissance pile, only two are exactly alike. *Lauriston Place.*

⑫ **The Vennel.** Near the top of the steep steps on this footpath ('vennel' is a Scots word that translates as alley) is a section of the Flodden Wall (marked with a sign), indicating how areas well below the castle's rocky perch, such as the Grassmarket, were enclosed within a fortified city by the 16th century. *Heriot Place, at Keir St.*

⑬ ★ **Grassmarket.** This was once a market square and a place for executions. One of the most infamous was of Margaret Dickson or 'Poor Maggie' as she was nick-named after being convicted for having a baby out of wedlock. After she was duly hanged in 1724, her body was en route to burial when her escorts heard a banging in the coffin. Maggie was alive and, according to one version of the tale, lived another 40 years. A bar in Grassmarket is named in her honor. *See also p 20,* ⑨.

New **Town**

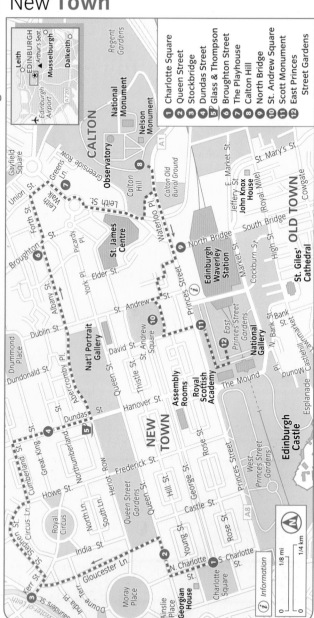

1 Charlotte Square
2 Queen Street
3 Stockbridge
4 Dundas Street
5 Glass & Thompson
6 Broughton Street
7 The Playhouse
8 Calton Hill
9 North Bridge
10 St. Andrew Square
11 Scott Monument
12 East Princes Street Gardens

EDINBURGH
Leith
Arthur's Seat
Musselburgh
Edinburgh Airport
A720
Dalkeith

Regent Gardens

National Monument

CALTON

Nelson Monument

Observatory

Greenside Row

Gayfield Square

Union St.
Forth St.
St.
Leith Walk
Greens Ln.

Broughton St.
Picardy Pl.
York Pl.
Elder St.
Albany St.

St. James Centre

Leith St.

Calton Hill

Calton Old Burial Ground

A1

Waterloo Pl.

North Bridge

Edinburgh Waverley Station

St. Mary's St.

E. Market St.
Jeffery St.
John Knox House
(Royal Mile)
South Bridge
Market St.
Cockburn St.
High St.
Cowgate

OLD TOWN

St. Giles' Cathedral

Dublin St.
Drummond Place
Dundonald St.

Nat'l Portrait Gallery

David St.
Queen St.
Thistle St.

St. Andrew Square

St. Andrew St.

Princes Street

East Princes Street Gardens

N. Bank St.
S. Bank St.

National Gallery

The Mound

Castlehill
Lawnmarket
Mound Pl.

Abercromby Pl.

Cumberland St.
Great King St.
Northumberland St.
Heriot Row

Assembly Rooms
Royal Scottish Academy

Hanover St.

NEW TOWN

Rose St.

George St.

Esplanade

Edinburgh Castle

Kerr St.
St. Stephen St.
St. Stephen Circus Ln.

Howe St.
North Ln.
South Ln.
Queen Street Gardens
Queen St.

Hill St.
George St.
Castle St.
Rose St.

West Princes Street Gardens

India St.

Royal Circus

Frederick St.
Young St.

Princes Street Gardens

A8

Gloucester Ln.

Ainslie Place
Moray Place

Doune Terr.
India Pl.
Water of Leith
Saunders St.

N. Charlotte St.
S. Charlotte St.

Charlotte Square

Georgian House

(i) Information

0   1/8 mi
0   1/4 km

N

In 1767, the city fathers realized that the best way to relieve the increasingly cramped and unhygienic Old Town was to create a New Town. It is perhaps the definitive example of rational Georgian town planning, with new roads laid out in a strict grid. With subsequent additions, Edinburgh's New Town became a city center with fine housing, offices, and commercial space. START: **West end of George St.**

1 ★ **Charlotte Square.** This is actually the final part of the first New Town, designed by the preeminent Georgian-era architect Robert Adam in 1791, just before his death. The central park was subsequently transformed from a circle into an octagon in 1873, and a statue of Prince Albert was added. On the north side find **The Georgian House** (p 23, **1**) as well as **Bute House,** the official residence of the Scottish First Minister. *See p 14,* **7**.

2 ★ **Queen Street.** This northernmost street of the original New Town development has the area's largest number of original buildings. As on Princes Street, townhouses were built only on one side of what is today a very busy boulevard, with the private **Queen Street Gardens** running opposite. On a clear day, you can see right across northern

Edinburgh to Leith, the Firth of Forth, and Fife in the distance. *Queen St., at N. Castle St.*

3 ★★ **Stockbridge.** This charming neighborhood's name comes from the Stock Bridge which crosses the Water of Leith. The district was a hippy enclave in the '60s and '70s, but is now a refuge of the well-heeled. Deanhaugh Street serves as the local main street and St. Stephen Street has a variety of places to shop and eat. *See p 15,* **10**.

4 ★ **Dundas Street.** With the first New Town completed, a Northern version was planned at the beginning of the 19th century by architects Robert Reid and William Sibbald. Northern New Town wasn't built in a day, however. Land for the development was first acquired around the 1790s, but buildings

The central park in Charlotte Square during the Edinburgh Book Festival.

were still being added as late as the 1850s. Dundas Street is at its core, and if you like antiques it's worth coming here for some window-shopping at least. *Dundas St., at Great King St.*

5 ★ **Glass & Thompson** is a classic, upscale cafe that feels part and parcel of Edinburgh's rather up-market New Town. Platters feature a mix of local and Continental ingredients, cheese, seafood, cold meats, and salad. Open until late afternoon. *2 Dundas St.* ☎ *0131/557-0909. £.*

6 ★ **Broughton Street.** Broughton Street is central to the city's gay scene. At the top of the road, near the large and busy roundabout, is the short street called Picardy Place. Picardy is what this area was once called, the land being acquired in 1730 for a group of French silk weavers. Their attempts to grow mulberry trees for the silkworms, however, didn't work. Broughton Street is one of the key destinations

The opulant Playhouse theatre.

for nightlife in Edinburgh, home to traditional pubs and stylish bars. *Broughton St., at Picardy Place.*

7 ★ **The Playhouse.** Here, at the top of Leith Walk, this opulent theater was designed (1927–29) by Glasgow architect John Fairweather (1867–1942) for films and theater productions. While it appears to be only two stories high from the front, the land behind the facade drops off and the interior space fills several more floors. Fairweather was inspired by a trip to the US and the auditorium was designed to hold more than 3,000 people—huge in its day. *See p 100.*

8 ★★★ **Calton Hill.** Check out Robert Louis Stevenson's favorite spot for gazing at the city. *See p 9,* **2**.

9 ★ **North Bridge.** This is an excellent vantage point for viewing Edinburgh Castle. Curiously, like this elevated crossing, few of the city's many bridges actually cross water; they link hills instead. The first North Bridge took some 9 years to complete from 1763. The current broad span was built from 1894 to 1897, soaring over railway lines and Waverley Station below. *At Princes St.*

10 **St. Andrew Square.** Named for the patron saint of Scotland, this square is the eastern bookend to Charlotte Square (**1**) due west. Alas, it doesn't carry the same Georgian character, as redevelopment has introduced some negligible architecture. Atop the 38m (125-ft.) column (modeled on Trajan's Column in Rome) in the middle of the square's gated garden stands Lord Melville (1742–1811), once one of Scotland's most powerful politicians. *George St., at St. David St.*

Scott Monument.

the monument's commissioning committee he got the job. Never mind the Victorian critic John Ruskin's rather harsh review or the slightly dodgy process—the Gothic shrine remains one of the most notable landmarks in the city. *East Princes St. Gardens, near Waverley Station.* ☎ *0131/529-4068. www. cac.org.uk. Admission £3. Daily Apr–Sept 10am–6pm; Oct–Mar 10am–3pm. Bus: 3, 12, 25, 33, or 45.*

⓫ ★ **Scott Monument.** George Meikle Kemp (1795–1844), a carpenter by trade, was actually third in the competition to create the tribute to Sir Walter Scott, but after prolonged discussions by

⓬ ★★ **East Princes Street Gardens.** It took many years to completely drain the old Nor' Loch that once covered this area, and the 3.4-hectare (8.5-acre) park that now fills the valley was begun in 1830. The original designs for the park, however, had to be altered in the wake of the construction of the railway lines into Waverley Station. The panoramic views of Old Town rising to Ramsay Gardens and Edinburgh Castle are excellent from here. *The southern end of Princes Street, running from The Mound to Waverley Station.*

Fountain in Princes Street Gardens.

Leith

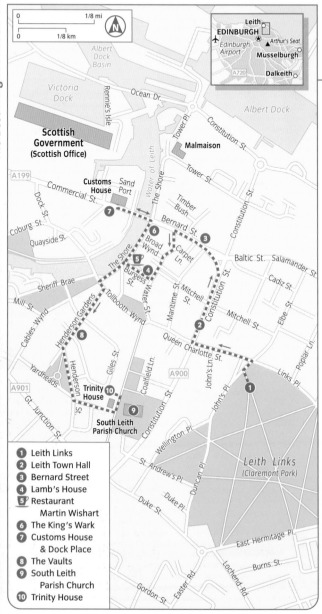

1 Leith Links
2 Leith Town Hall
3 Bernard Street
4 Lamb's House
5 Restaurant
  Martin Wishart
6 The King's Wark
7 Customs House
  & Dock Place
8 The Vaults
9 South Leith
  Parish Church
10 Trinity House

Edinburgh's long-standing port at Leith takes advantage of a natural harbor where the little Water of Leith fed into the massive Firth of Forth estuary. Only properly incorporated into Edinburgh's city limits in the 20th century, Leith has long had its own identity and it was effectively Scotland's capital during the interim rule of Mary of Guise in the 16th century. START: **John's Place. Bus: 12, 16, or 35.**

1 ★ **Leith Links.** Older than Bruntsfield Links golf course on the Meadows (p 20, **10**), Leith Links is by some accounts the birthplace of golf. A version of the sport was first played here in the 1400s, but it wasn't until 1744 that the first rules of the game were laid down. Today it's a pleasant public park with no golf allowed, but running adjacent to John's Place is the fairway of this ancient course's first hole. *East of John's Place, between Duke St. and Links Gardens. Free admission. Daily dawn–dusk. Bus: 12, 16, or 35.*

2 **Leith Town Hall.** This neoclassical building was originally constructed as Leith's Sheriff Court in 1828. The designers' firm is emblazoned on the Queen Charlotte Street frontage: 'R. & R. Dickson'. The adjoining property was incorporated later after the town became a parliamentary burgh in 1833. *75–81 Constitution St. and 29–41 Queen Charlotte St.*

3 ★ **Bernard Street.** This short road feels more like a square than a street, lined with a mix of Georgian and 19th-century commercial buildings, including the former **Leith Bank.** At its eastern end, where Bernard meets Constitution Street, is another of Scotland's many monuments to poet Robert Burns—a bronze statue, erected in 1898. At this corner you can also see the Leith **Assembly Rooms** (37–43 Constitution St.). The building includes a merchants' meeting place built in the 1780s and a ballroom.

4 ★★ **Lamb's House.** A wander up Carpet Lane takes you to this handsome, red-tile-roofed building. Originally a large early 17th-century merchant's house (the finest example of its type in Edinburgh), Lamb's House is a masterpiece of architecture, with crow-stepped gables and corbels. Rumor has it a ghost or two haunt the place. *Burgess St. and Water St.*

5 ★★★ **Restaurant Martin Wishart** is arguably the finest restaurant in the city and one of three in Leith with the highest accolades in the UK. Lunch is not too expensive considering the quality, at around £30 for the three-course set price meal. Reservations are a must. *See p 80. £££.*

Leith Links was originally used as a golf course.

6 ★ **The King's Wark.** This building dates to the beginning of the 1700s and has a rich history. The original King's Wark on this site (around 1434) was believed to be a palace and arsenal that King James VI had rebuilt during his reign in the 17th century, and was later given to a tavern-keeping buddy of his, Bernard Lindsay. It now houses a pub, one of many welcoming options on The Shore, Leith's first main street. *36 The Shore.*

7 ★ **Customs House & Dock Place.** Designed by Robert Reid in 1810, the Customs House is quite a monumental (if somewhat harsh) building, with its sturdy fluted columns. Look out for the royal arms of King George III in the triangular pediment that rests on the columns. Nearby is the original entrance to the Old East Dock: The **Commercial Quay,** established at the start of the 19th century and today redeveloped with shops and restaurants, including the award-winning **Kitchin** (see p 78). *Commercial St., at Dock Place.*

8 ★ **The Vaults.** This handsome and broad stone warehouse dates back to 1682, but the vaulted passage and wine cellar underneath

The columns of Customs House.

Restaurant Martin Wishart.

may be around 100 years older. Leith is where scores of bottles of French wine were imported, and the word 'claret' is believed by some to be one that Scots gave to red wine from Bordeaux. A link to that history is maintained by the **Vintners Rooms** restaurant here (p 82). The **Scotch Malt Whisky Society** is located on the second floor. *87 Giles St.*

9 **South Leith Parish Church.** Although a church has been standing at this site since around 1480, the current structure was built much later in 1848. A plaque in the kirkyard details the intervening history, which includes some very heavy bombardment in 1560 by English troops and Oliver Cromwell's later decision to use the poor, ravaged church as a munitions hold. *6 Henderson St.*

10 **Trinity House.** Trinity House is an early 1800s survivor amid the urban renewal and tall apartment buildings of central Leith. Owned by Historic Scotland, it is home to the **Incorporation of Shipmasters,** an organization that dates to the 14th century. *99 Kirkgate.* ☎ *0131/554-3289. Group tours by reservation.* ●

54

The Best Shopping

Edinburgh Shopping

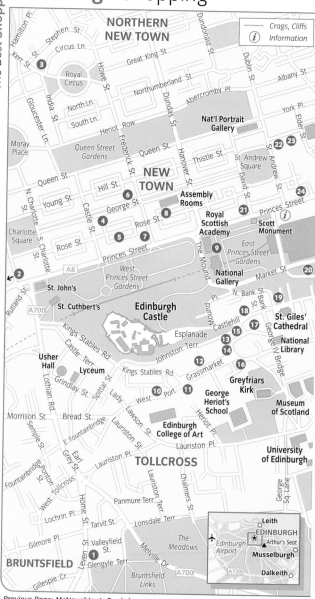

Crags, Cliffs

(i) Information

NORTHERN NEW TOWN

Hamilton Pl.

Stephen St.

Circus Ln.

Kerr St.

Royal Circus

Howe St.

Great King St.

Dundonald St.

Dublin St.

Albany St.

India St.

Gloucester Ln.

North Ln.

South Ln.

Heriot Row

Northumberland St.

Abercromby Pl.

Dundas St.

York Pl.

Elder St.

Moray Place

Queen Street Gardens

Frederick St.

Queen St.

Nat'l Portrait Gallery

St. Andrew Square

22 23

N. Charlotte St.

Young St.

Hill St.

George St.

6

Rose St.

8

NEW TOWN

Hanover St.

Thistle St.

Assembly Rooms

Royal Scottish Academy

21

David St.

St. Andrew St.

24

Princes Street

i

Charlotte Square

S. Charlotte St.

Castle St.

4

5

7

Rose St.

Princes Street

A8

West Princes Street Gardens

9

Scott Monument

East Princes Street Gardens

Market St.

20

Rutland St.

A700

St. John's

St. Cuthbert's

Edinburgh Castle

The Mound

National Gallery

N. Bank St.

S. Bank St.

18

Castlehill

19

St. Giles' Cathedral

2

Kings Stables Rd

Esplanade

13

15

17

George IV Bridge

National Library

Usher Hall

Castle Terr.

Lyceum

Johnston Terr.

14

16

Grassmarket

Greyfriars Kirk

Museum of Scotland

Grindlay St.

Spittal

Lady Lawson St.

West Port

10

11

George Heriot's School

Heriot Pl.

Morrison St.

Bread St.

Lothian Rd.

E. Fountainbridge

Lauriston St.

Edinburgh College of Art

Lauriston Pl.

University of Edinburgh

George Sq. Lane

Semple St.

Fountainbridge

Ponton St.

Earl Grey St.

West Tollcross

Lauriston Pl.

TOLLCROSS

Lauriston Terr.

Chalmers St.

Home St.

Lochrin Pl.

Tarvit St.

Panmure Terr.

Lonsdale Terr.

Gilmore Pl.

Valleyfield St.

Melville Dr.

The Meadows

Leith

EDINBURGH

Arthur's Seat

Edinburgh Airport

Musselburgh

BRUNTSFIELD

Glengyle Terr.

1

Bruntsfield Links

A700

A720

Dalkeith

Gillespie Cr.

Previous Page: McNaughtan's Bookshop.

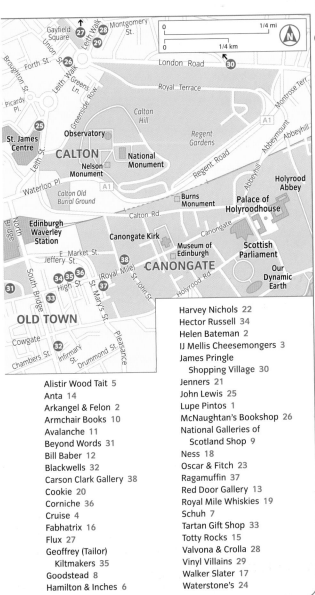

Shopping Best Bets

Best **Italian Deli**
★★ Valvona & Crolla, *19 Elm Row (p 60)*

Best **Cheesemonger**
★★★ IJ Mellis Cheesemongers, *Bakers Place (Kerr St., p 59)*

Best **Kilts**
★ Geoffrey (Tailor) Kiltmakers, *57–59 High St. (p 61)*

Best **Woolen Jumpers**
★ Ragamuffin, *276 Canongate (p 61)*

Best **Foot Forward**
Schuh, *6 Frederick St. (p 62)*

Best **Men's Fashions**
★★ Walker Slater, *20 Victoria St. (p 58)*

Best for **Designer Labels**
Arkangel & Felon, *4 William St. (p 57)*

Best for **Womenswear**
★ Corniche, *2 Jeffrey St. (p 58)*

Best for **Urban Chic**
★ Cruise, *94 George St. (p 58)*

Best **Unique Gift**
★★ Carson Clark Gallery, *181 Canongate (p 57)*

Best for **Knickknacks**
Tartan Gift Shop, *54 High St. (p 60)*

Best **Fashion Jewelry**
Hamilton & Inches, *87 George St. (p 61)*

Best for **Antiquarian Books**
★★ McNaughtan's Bookshop, *3a Haddington Place (p 57)*

Best **Book Selection**
★ Waterstone's, *128 Princes St. (p 57)*

Best **Department Store**
★★ John Lewis, *St. James Centre (p 59)*

Best for **Keeping Your Head Warm**
★★ Fabhatrix, *13 Cowgatehead (p 60)*

Best for **Scottish Crafts**
★ Ness, *336 Lawnmarket (p 58)*

Best **Whisky Shop**
★★★ Royal Mile Whiskies, *379 High St. (p 62)*

IJ Mellis cheesemongers.

Edinburgh **Shopping A to Z**

Bookworms will delight in the second-hand books at Mcnaughtan's.

Antiques

★★ Carson Clark Gallery OLD TOWN   Specialists in historic maps rather than modern OS versions, you'll find a selection of original 16th- to 19th-century antique maps and sea charts from all over the world here. An ideal place to source a gift perhaps. *181 Canongate.* ☎ *0131/556-4710. www.carson clarkgallery.co.uk. MC, V. Bus: 35. Map p 54.*

Books

Armchair Books WEST END West of the Grassmarket, and split over two buildings, this charming, eclectic secondhand bookshop is packed high with everything from fiction, poetry, and local history to antiquarian tomes. *72 and 74 West Port* ☎ *0131/229-5927. www. armchairbooks.co.uk. MC, V. Bus: 2 or 35. Map p 54.*

Beyond Words OLD TOWN   One of the best independent bookshops in the UK, this store specializes in beautiful coffee table photography books, covering art, cinema, fashion, nature, travel, and more. Some related magazines are also available. *42–44 Cockburn St.* ☎ *0131/ 226-6636. www.beyondwords.co.uk. MC, V. Bus: 35. Map p 54.*

Blackwells OLD TOWN   A stone's throw from the Royal Mile, this popular chain-bookstore, best-known for academic titles, has a knowledgeable staff and wide-ranging shelves of fiction and nonfiction. *53 South Bridge.* ☎ *0131/622-8222. www.blackwells.com. AE, MC, V. Bus: 3, 7, 30, or 37. Map p 54.*

★★ McNaughtan's Bookshop NEW TOWN   In business since the late 1950s, this is one of the city's best antiquarian and secondhand book purveyors. A must stop for literature lovers. *3a Haddington Place (Leith Walk, near Gayfield Sq.).* ☎ *0131/556-5897. www. mcnaughtansbookshop.com. MC, V. Bus: 7, 12, 16, or 22. Map p 54.*

★ Waterstone's NEW TOWN   A giant Barnes-and-Noble-like operation, with plenty of reading options and soft seats. This is the most prominent and best-stocked book retailer in the city center. *128 Princes St. (across from Waverley Station).* ☎ *0131/226-2666. AE, MC, V. Bus: 8, 22, 25, 33. Map p 54.*

Clothing

Arkangel & Felon WEST END William Street, in the city's affluent West End, is home to a host of boutique shops. A & F specializes in exclusive designer labels and brands such as Anton Heunis and

Head to Arkangel for designer labels.

American Vintage. *4 William St.* ☎ *0131/226-4466. www.arkangel andfelon.com. MC, V. Bus: 4 or 25. Map p 54.*

Cookie OLD TOWN   As would be expected on Cockburn Street, this quirky shop has a mixture of tees from the likes of Ruby Walk and Sugarhill—all reasonably priced. Look out for the printed cotton summer dresses, which are perfect for the festival season. *29 Cockburn St.* ☎ *0131/622-7260. MC, V. Bus: 35. Map p 54.*

★ **Corniche** OLD TOWN   One of the more sophisticated boutiques in Edinburgh; if it's the latest in fashion, expect to find it here. Brands for men include Comme des Garçons or Pauline Burrows: For women Et Compagnie or Vivienne Westwood Anglomania. *2 Jeffrey St. (near the Royal Mile).* ☎ *0131/556-3707. www.corniche.org.uk. AE, MC, V. Bus: 35. Map p 54.*

★ **Cruise** NEW TOWN   This homegrown outlet began in Edinburgh's Old Town. There is still a branch off the Royal Mile, but the New Town outlet is the focus for couture. The A to Z of fashion stretches from Acne slim-fit jeans to Y-3 trainers. *94 George St.* ☎ *0131/226-3524. www. cruiseclothing.co.uk. MC, V. Bus: 19, 37, or 41. Map p 54.*

Goodstead NEW TOWN   Come here for casual, ultra-trendy men's and women's branded clothes and accessories. Shop for Farah pin-stripe shorts or Norse Project sailor knits for him, or Swedish biker jackets and pretty French frocks for her. *76 Rose St.* ☎ *0131/228-2846. www.goodstead.co.uk. MC, V. Bus:10,12,16,23, or 27. Map p 54.*

★ **Ness** OLD TOWN   A feminine collection of women's knitwear, skirts, T-shirts, and accessories (shoes, bags, and purses) scoured from around the country—from the Orkney Islands to the Borders. *336 Lawnmarket.* ☎ *0131/225-8815. www.nessbypost.com. MC, V. Bus: 28. Map p 54.*

Totty Rocks OLD TOWN   Established by two graduates from the Edinburgh School of Art who have since worked in London, Milan, and Hong Kong, this shop features their own contemporary womenswear collection, alongside other selective labels. Prices are not cheap. *40 Victoria St.* ☎ *0131/226-3232. www. tottyrocks.com. MC, V. Bus: 35, 41, or 42. Map p 54.*

★★ **Walker Slater** OLD TOWN   Well-made and contemporary (if understated) men's clothes, usually made of cotton and dyed in rich, earthy hues. Also carries Mackintosh overcoats and accessories. *20 Victoria St. (near George IV Bridge).* ☎ *0131/220-2636. www.walker slater.com. MC, V. Bus: 35, 41, or 42. Map p 54.*

Department Stores
★ **Harvey Nichols** NEW TOWN   The place to come for up-market clothes, accessories and general goods, this store's multiple floors include high-end fashion by the likes of Jimmy Choo and Alexander McQueen. *30–34 St. Andrew Sq.* ☎ *0131/524-8388. www.harveynichols.com.*

Vintage Racks

Thanks in part to a large student population, Edinburgh is rather rich in vintage clothes outlets. Among the best is the **Rusty Zip** (14 Teviot Pl. ☎ 0131/226 4634). This retro clothing outlet packs a lot in, whether cool vintage items or cheesy retro accessories. Larger sister outlet is **Armstrong's** at 80 Grassmarket (☎ 0131/220-5557). Also consider **Elaine's Vintage Clothes** in Stockbridge, where the owner is often on hand to advise shoppers (55 St. Stephen St. ☎ 0131/225-5783), or **Herman Brown,** which specializes in women's and gent's togs from the 1940s to present (151 West Port ☎ 0131/228-2589). A newcomer to the city is **The Frayed Hem** (45 Cockburn St. ☎ 0131/225-9831), with furs, tuxes, and silk shirts. Just outside the city in the coastal town of Portobello is newcomer **Urban Igloo** (240a High St., Portobello ☎ 0788/271-3641), which specializes in 'up-cycled' (adapted) clothing alongside the usual retro goods.

AE, MC, V. Bus: 8, 12, 17, or 45. Map p 54.

Jenners NEW TOWN   This neo-Gothic landmark opened in 1838 and since 2005 has been part of the House of Fraser chain. It sells a variety of international and local merchandise alongside an array of gift-oriented Scottish products in the food hall. *48 Princes St. ☎ 0870/607-2841. www. houseoffraser.co.uk. AE, MC, V. Bus: 8, 22, 25, or 33. Map p 54.*

★★ John Lewis NEW TOWN   The largest department store in Scotland, John Lewis is many people's first choice when it comes to shopping. Well-known for good quality, own-label and popular branded clothes, appliances, furniture, toys, and more. *St. James Centre (at the top of Leith Walk). ☎ 0131/556-9121. www.johnlewis.com. AE, MC, V. Bus: 7, 14, 22, or 25. Map p 54.*

Food & Wine
★★★ IJ Mellis Cheesemongers STOCKBRIDGE   This is the place to come for award-winning British and Irish cheeses. Helpful staff is always on-hand to offer advice here and at the two other stores in the city (see website for details). *6 Bakers Place (Kerr St.). ☎ 0131/225-6566. www. mellischeese.co.uk. MC, V. Bus: 24, 29, or 42. Map p 54.*

★ Lupe Pintos WEST END   This small shop in the Tollcross neighborhood specializes in Mexican

Inventive display at Harvey Nichols.

HARVEY NICHOLS

Pick up your picnic at Valvona & Crolla.

food, but also stocks US goods, as well as exotic treats from the Far East, such as Indonesian roast chicken seasoning or red and green curry paste. *24 Leven St. (near the King's Theatre).* ☎ *0131/228-6241. www.lupepintos.com. MC, V. Bus: 11, 15, or 45. Map p 54.*

★★ **Valvona & Crolla** NEW TOWN This Italian deli has an excellent reputation across the UK thanks to its wonderful selection of cheeses and cured meats, and baked goods from rolls to sourdough loaves. *19 Elm Row (Leith Walk).* ☎ *0131/556-6066. www. valvonacrolla.co.uk. MC, V. Bus: 7, 14, 22, or 25. Map p 54.*

Gifts
Flux LEITH A modestly sized shop in the heart of Leith, Flux sells Scottish crafts, ethically conscious gifts, and handmade cards. It provides some appealing alternatives to the tacky souvenirs widely available. *55 Bernard St.* ☎ *0131/554-4075. www.get2flux. co.uk. MC, V. Bus: 16. Map p 54.*

National Galleries of Scotland Shop NEW TOWN Custom prints of the best of the country's art collection, books, and other gifts—this shop in the Weston Link below the main gallery and Royal Scottish Academy is well worth a visit. *Weston Link, Princes Street Gardens.*

☎ *0131/624-6200. www.national galleries.org. AE, MC, V. Bus:1, 22, 25, 33, or 44. Map p 54.*

★ **Red Door Gallery** OLD TOWN A boutique store dedicated to selling art and design by local talents. A well-chosen selection of books, cards, and accessories sit alongside affordable, original artworks and prints. *42 Victoria St.* ☎ *0131/477-3255. www.edinburgh art.com. MC, V. Bus: 35, 41, or 42. Map p 54.*

Tartan Gift Shop OLD TOWN A bewildering array of hunt and dress tartans for men and women, sold by the yard. There's also a line of lamb's wool and cashmere sweaters and all the proper kilt accessories. *54 High St.* ☎ *0131/558-3187. MC, V. Bus 35. Map p 54.*

Hats
★★ **Fabhatrix** OLD TOWN I'm partial to hats and this shop has hundreds of handmade ones: Practical and attractive options as well as a few that are downright frivolous but extremely fun. *13 Cowgatehead (off Grassmarket).* ☎ *0131/225-9222. www.fabhatrix.com. MC, V. Bus: 2. Map p 54.*

Jewelry
Alistir Wood Tait NEW TOWN A family-run business with a good

reputation for Scottish pearls and gemstones, including the rare Cairngorm quartz. Those interested in vintage should seek out the antique pieces, although these do not come cheap. *116A Rose St. ☎ 0131/225-4105. www.alistirtaitgem.co.uk. MC, V. Bus: 19. Map p 54.*

Hamilton & Inches NEW

TOWN Since 1866, the prestigious Hamilton & Inches has sold gold and silver jewelry, porcelain, silver, and gift items. The company has its own silver workshops and holds a Royal Warrant. *87 George St. ☎ 0131/225-4898. www.hamiltonandinches.com. AE, MC, V. Bus: 19 or 41. Map p 54.*

Kilts & Tartans

Anta OLD TOWN Along with stylish tartan clothing for the whole family, Anta has cozy wool and cashmere throws, cushions, luggage (including both overnight bags and handbags), and gorgeous painted tableware. *Crocket's Land, 91–93 West Bow. ☎ 0131/225-4616. www.anta.co.uk. MC, V. Bus: 35, 41, or 42. Map p 54.*

★ Geoffrey (Tailor) Kiltmakers

OLD TOWN Past customers of this renowned kiltmakers have included Dr. Ruth Westheimer and Mel Gibson

Stylish headwear at Fabhatrix.

(who apparently favors the 'Hunting Buchanan' tartan). They stock 200 of Scotland's best-known clan patterns. *57–59 High St. ☎ 0131/557-0256. www.geoffreykilts.co.uk. MC, V. Bus: 35. Map p 54.*

Hector Russell OLD TOWN A

bespoke (or made-to-measure) service can be acquired at this well-respected Highland-based kiltmaker, with shops on the Royal Mile and Princes Street. A typical kilt of heavy-weight 10-yard wool will set you back about £300. *137–141 High St. ☎ 0131/558-1254. www.hector-russell.com. MC, V. Bus: 35. Map p 54.*

James Pringle Shopping Vil-

lage LEITH The Leith mill for this well-known Inverness-based weaver produces a large variety of wool items and boasts a clan ancestry center with a database containing more than 50,000 family names. *70–74 Bangor Rd. ☎ 0131/553-5161. MC, V. Bus: 36. Map p 54.*

Knits & Woolens

Bill Baber OLD TOWN This workshop and store turns out modernized adaptations of Scottish knit patterns for women. Designs are handmade using a variety of organic and natural fibers, including silk and linen. *66 Grassmarket. ☎ 0131/225-3249. www.billbaber.com. MC, V. Bus: 2. Map p 54.*

★ Ragamuffin OLD TOWN A

source of unique 'wearable art' created by some 150 UK-based designers including Sophie's Wild Woollens of Cumbria and Quernstone Knitwear's casual, natural tops from Stromness on Orkney. *276 Canongate. ☎ 0131/557-6007. www.ragamuffinonline.co.uk. MC, V. Bus: 35. Map p 54.*

Music

★ **Avalanche** OLD TOWN This excellent indie music shop has been trading in the city center for over 20 years, and is the place to go for new releases of Scottish bands as well as secondhand vinyl and CDs. You can also buy gig tickets here. *5 Grassmarket* ☎ *0131 659 7708. www. avalancherecords.co.uk. MC, V. Bus: 2. Map p 54.*

Vinyl Villains NEW TOWN Stop by this independent music store to look through their wide selection of collectable LPs, music books, CDs, and DVDs—of all genres from heavy metal to soundtracks. *5 Elm Row (Leith Walk)* ☎ *0131/558-1170. www.vinylvillains.co.uk. MC, V. Bus: 14, 29, 31, or 47. Map p 54.*

Shoes
Helen Bateman WEST END
Slinky slings and sandals to sensible driving loafers and some devilish red suede pumps, Ms Bateman offers her own line of fashionable women's shoes. Most shoes have matching handbags too. *16 William St.* ☎ *0131/220-4495. www.helen bateman.com. MC, V. Bus: 12, 25, 33, or 44. Map p 54.*

Schuh NEW TOWN Come to this trend-conscious shoe store for spangly, party heels from Red or

Dead, everyday comfy flats by the likes of Rocket Dog, and ever popular trainer brands such as Converse. *6 Frederick St.* ☎ *0131/220-0290. www.schuh.co.uk. MC, V. Bus: 19, 29, or 42. Map p 54.*

Spectacles
Oscar & Fitch NEW TOWN
Tucked behind the Edinburgh branch of Harvey Nichols is this equally fashionable shop for designer eyewear and oversized shades worthy of the world's leading celebrities. *20 Multrees Walk, St. Andrew Sq.* ☎ *0131/556-6461. www.oscarandfitch.com. AE, MC, V. Bus: 15, 42, or 67. Map p 54.*

Whisky
★★★ Royal Mile Whiskies OLD TOWN The choice at this rather small shop on the Royal Mile is huge: Some 1,000 different Scotch and worldwide-sourced whiskies are available. The staff is very knowledgeable, so don't hesitate to ask for advice. *379 High St.* ☎ *0131/ 622-6255. www.royalmile whiskies.com. AE, MC, V. Bus: 35. Map p 54.* ●

The Macabre Market

It is no surprise that Edinburgh, a city rife with ghost tours and a history of some bizarre crimes, has a bunch of spooky shops too. Head to the **Black Mausoleum** (19 Candlemaker Row, ☎ 0131/ 226-7500), which has a link to the **City of the Dead Tours** (www. blackhart.uk.com), and sells creepy handmade gifts and original artwork. Sister store **The Creepy Wee Shop** is only a few steps over the road, in the allegedly haunted Greyfriars Kirkyard (28b Candlemaker Row, ☎ 0131/225-9044). **The Cadies & Witchery Tours** shop (84 West Bow ☎ 0131/225-6745) is the place for souvenir skulls and dragons, whilst **Voodoo** (34 Cockburn St. ☎ 0131/622-7318) will kit you out with a gothic wardrobe.

The Great Outdoors

Arthur's Seat

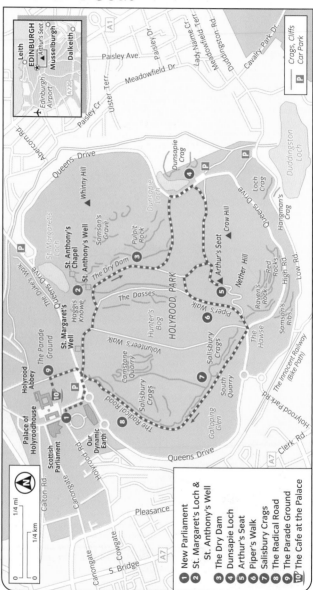

Crags, Cliffs

P Car Park

EDINBURGH
Leith
Arthur's Seat
Musselburgh
Dalkeith
Edinburgh Airport
A720

1. New Parliament
2. St. Margaret's Loch & St. Anthony's Well
3. The Dry Dam
4. Dunsapie Loch
5. Arthur's Seat
6. Piper's Walk
7. Salisbury Crags
8. The Radical Road
9. The Parade Ground
10. The Cafe at the Palace

Princes Street Gardens.

The most invigorating of Edinburgh's outdoor escapes lies quite literally at the doorstep of Old Town. Holyrood Park is home to Arthur's Seat, and a climb to the top of this landmark hill provides some of the best views in the region. Allow about 2 hours to get to the top of Arthur's Seat and back using this tour. START: Take Bus 35 or 36 to Holyrood Lodge Information Centre.

1 New Parliament. The pleasant if slightly exposed urban park at the New Scottish Parliament uses modern landscape design, with reflecting pools and tiers of concrete benches, surrounded by low-maintenance grasses and wildflowers in summer. Look up toward Arthur's Seat to glimpse ant-size people walking about the peak. 🕐 *20 min.*

A statue inside the Parliament grounds.

Adjacent to Scottish Parliament, on the bottom of Royal Mile, opposite the Palace of Holyroodhouse.

2 ★ St. Margaret's Loch & St. Anthony's Well. Named for St. Margaret (1045–93), the pious queen consort to King Malcolm III, this large, pleasant pond teems with bird life. Near the ruins of **St. Anthony's Chapel** (whose history is somewhat fuzzy, though it definitely dates back to the 15th century), on the stony bluff above the loch, the path runs past a boulder and smaller rock basin marking St. Anthony's Well. 🕐 *10 min. Just south of Queens Dr.*

The modern landscaping of the parliament grounds.

What's in a Name?

Many presume that Arthur's Seat is a reference to the mythical king of Camelot. Not so. There are various theories behind the name. The moniker may have come from a 6th-century prince of Strathclyde named Arthur, or it could be a corruption of 'archer', given the hill's defensive position. My pick is that it's a bastardization of Gaelic for the height of Thor, or 'Ard Thor'.

❸ ★ The Dry Dam. This rutted trail (along a glacial cirque, or valley) takes you straight toward Arthur's Seat, clearly the highest peak amid the other hilltops and ridgelines. Take a rest and catch your breath. Be sure to look behind you for views of **Calton Hill** to the left and the Hiberian football park in the direction of Leith and the River Forth. ⏱ *10 min.*

❹ ★★ Dunsapie Loch. From a ridge above this man-made loch (created in 1844), you'll get a good panorama looking north across the firth to Fife—and east to the coastal towns of East Lothian. On a sunny day, the eastern horizon reveals the dark cone of **North Berwick Law**, some 30km (19 miles) away, as well as shimmering silvery **Bass Rock**, the famous bird sanctuary in the sea. Just below the loch is terrain believed to be ancient farmlands. ⏱ *15 min. Where Dry Dam joins Piper's Walk.*

❺ ★★★ Arthur's Seat. You are now standing atop a long-dormant volcano, some 250m (820 ft.) above sea level. Don't be surprised if there's a howling gale blowing—my eyes water on every visit. Take time to soak up the 360-degree vista from this peak. There is a landmark indicator to help you identify the sights. Facing due north, Bass Rock is at 2 o'clock from your position. On the clearest day you can see as

far as **Ben Lomond** in the north-west (at about 10 o'clock), some 95km (59 miles) away. Take care as the rocks (polished by the soles of frequent visitors) can be slippery. ⏱ *30–45 min.*

❻ ★★ Piper's Walk. The Piper's Walk (the name commemorates a successful protest staged by the Highland troops—and their pipers—atop Arthur's Seat in 1778) is a narrow path below the summit, with prickly gorse bushes growing to your left amid rocky outcrops. The route offers a good view below of the **Hunter's Bog** (a haven for butterflies and moths) and another valley path called the Volunteer's Walk. ⏱ *20 min.*

❼ ★★ Salisbury Crags. As the southern part of Edinburgh comes into view (note the charming baronial-style stone buildings of the Pollok Hall student residences), you'll head under Salisbury Crags. Years of stone quarrying have revealed this bare but geologically significant facade of igneous rock. Climbing the 122m (400-ft.) edifice is discouraged. ⏱ *15 min. West side of Holyrood Park.*

❽ ★ The Radical Road. This trail offers good views of the **Pentlands Hills** in the distance and several city landmarks, including **Edinburgh Castle.** As you round the final bend, you'll get a good look at the gigantic white tent of **Our Dynamic Earth** and the arresting abstract geometry

Arthur's Seat

of the **Scottish Parliament** buildings. The name for the path allegedly stems from those who built it in the 1820s—unemployed artisans who fomented revolutionary ideas. Their political efforts failed, but they were given the task of constructing this road and the name's stuck ever since. ⏱ *15 min.*

⑨ The Parade Ground. This vast stretch of lawn is perfect for Frisbee or a ball game. In the mid-19th century, it was filled every August by scores of regiments on view for Queen Victoria (as well as 100,000 spectators) as part of the Royal Scottish Volunteer Review. ⏱ *15 min. North of Queen's Dr., east of Palace of Holyroodhouse.*

⑩ The Cafe at the Palace. After this hike, you deserve a break. Find the usual choice of drinks, snacks, cakes, and usually a few basic main meals, all homemade with locally sourced produce. Order at the counter and sit outside if the sun shines. *On the grounds of Holyrood Palace.* ☎ *0131/524-1032. £.*

Wordsworth on the Rock

The famous English poet William Wordsworth, along with his younger sister Dorothy and fellow writer Samuel Coleridge, toured Scotland at the beginning of the 19th century. Dorothy's memoirs were published as *Recollections of a Tour Made in Scotland, AD 1803*. The trio climbed Arthur's Seat on Friday, 6th September, and Dorothy notes: 'We set out on our walk . . . to the hill called Arthur's Seat, a high hill, very rocky at the top, and below covered with smooth turf. . . . We came to St. Anthony's Well and Chapel, as it is called, but it is more like a hermitage than a chapel—a small ruin . . . . We sate [sic] down on a stone not far from the chapel, overlooking a pastoral hollow as wild and solitary as any in the heart of the Highland mountains.'

Water of Leith

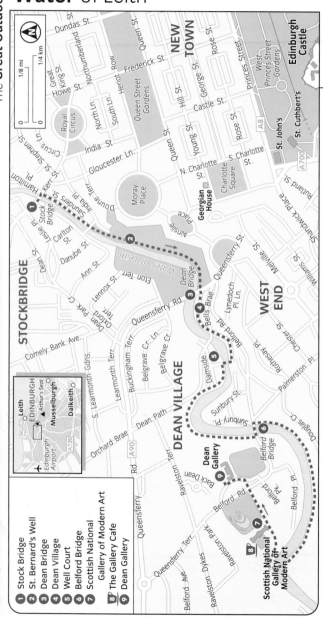

1 Stock Bridge
2 St. Bernard's Well
3 Dean Bridge
4 Dean Village
5 Well Court
7 Belford Bridge
7 Scottish National
Gallery of Modern Art
8 The Gallery Cafe
9 Dean Gallery

This relatively easy walk, just over an hour long, follows the small river—called the Water of Leith—that flows northeast on a meandering line through Edinburgh to the port of Leith. The trail includes the lovely Dean Village, often spelt *Dene* along the route, which is the older spelling and means 'deep valley'. START: **Water of Leith Walkway sign at the corner of Stockbridge and Saunders Streets.**

1 Stock Bridge. This crossing is the namesake of the surrounding neighborhood, previously a milling village. The bridge was first constructed in 1773 and later renovated, reconstructed, and widened—twice—in 1827 and 1901. As you follow the path southwest from the bridge (with the river on your right), you'll next come to **St. Bernard's Bridge** (around 1824) and its massive stone flight of stairs. ⏱ *10 min. Corner of Stockbridge and Saunders Sts.*

2 ★ St. Bernard's Well. Commissioned in 1788 to replace an earlier structure, this Romanesque domed temple contains a statue of *Hygeia*, the Greek goddess of good health. What you cannot see behind locked doors, alas, is the beautifully decorated interior of the pump room. ⏱ *10 min. At the banks of the Water of Leith.*

3 ★★★ Dean Bridge. One of the landmark design triumphs of the great engineer Thomas Telford (1757–1834). The four arches of this stone crossing rise magnificently from the ravine, ultimately soaring some 30m (almost 100 ft.) above the gently cascading riverbed below. It was constructed from 1831 to 1832, and was paid for by a former lord provost (mayor) who was redeveloping the lands of the former Dean estate. ⏱ *15 min. 200m/656 ft. past St. Bernard's Well; Queensferry Rd. (500m/1,640 ft. from city center).*

4 ★★★ Dean Village. Originally Water of Leith Village, this was a milling settlement that may date back to the 12th century. Admire the stonework on the yellow facade of the building at **Bell's Brae,** with its 17th-century panel of cherubs, scales, and milling imagery—as well

Red brick rooftops in Dean Village.

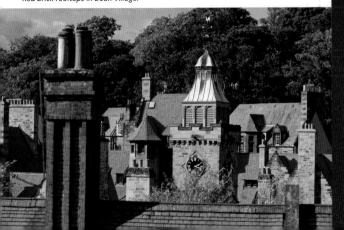

as a well-eroded inscription blessing the Baxters (bakers) of Edinburgh. The exposed half-timber construction of the **Hawthorn Buildings** dates to 1895. Wander to the middle of the low stone bridge (called the Old Bridge) that crosses the Water of Leith in the middle of the village for good river views. ⏱ *30 min. 1km/⅗-mile northwest of the city center, off Belford Rd.*

5 **Well Court.** This impressive baronial-style building, which housed apartments and a public hall, was built from 1883 to 1886 for the benefit of the community (whose milling business was going elsewhere). But the primary benefactor, newspaper owner Sir John Findlay, had an ulterior motive: The building made an attractive focal point from his home on the bluff above. ⏱ *10 min.*

6 **Belford Bridge.** Before you reach this single-arch stone bridge, you'll get a real sense of the depth of the gorge that the Water of Leith passes through as you walk along the wooded banks. The structure was completed in 1887 and has panels featuring the Edinburgh city coat of arms. ⏱ *15 min.*

7 **Scottish National Gallery of Modern Art.** The neoclassical building housing Scotland's National Gallery of Modern Art was formerly John Watson's School and dates to 1825. In front of the gallery, Landform was created in 2002. The spiraling banks of lawns, set around calm ponds, were designed by American landscape architect Charles Jencks. ⏱ *20 min. Belford Rd. Note that a gate from the river path up to the gallery grounds is locked at 6pm during the summer and at dusk during the winter. See p 28,* **5***.*

8 **The Gallery Cafe** at the National Gallery of Modern Art has a good deal of outdoor seating during the summer months, and serves freshly prepared ciabatta, salad, and soup. ☎ *0131/332-8600. £.*

9 **Dean Gallery.** On the grounds of this gallery is a sculpture (called Master of the Universe) by one of Scotland's most enduring modern/pop surrealist artists, Sir Eduardo Paolozzi (1924–2005). The gallery's neoclassical building dates back to 1831. The clock face on the front exterior was originally part of the old **Netherbow Port** near the World's End Close in the city's Old Town. Around the side is historic **Dean Cemetery,** which has some excellent examples of funerary monuments and sculpture. ⏱ *15 min. See p 18,* **1***.* ●

6 The Best **Dining**

Edinburgh Dining

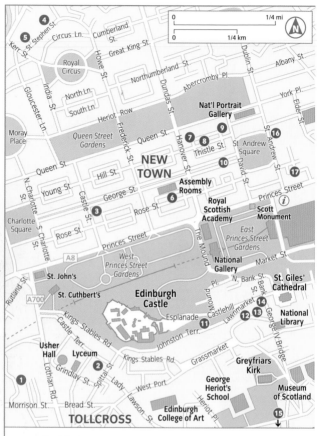

Barioja 21	Howies 13
Bell's Diner 5	Kebab Mahal 26
Café Royal Oyster Bar 17	La Garrigue 20
Café St. Honoré 7	Number One 18
Castle Terrace 2	Oloroso 3
David Bann 24	Ondine 14
The Dome Grill Room 10	Redwood 4
Dusit 8	Rhubarb 27
Forth Floor 16	Santini Ristorante 1
The Grain Store 12	Seadogs 6
Henderson's Vegetarian	Spoon Café Bistro 25
Restaurant 9	Sweet Melindas 15

Previous page: Café Royal's oyster bar.

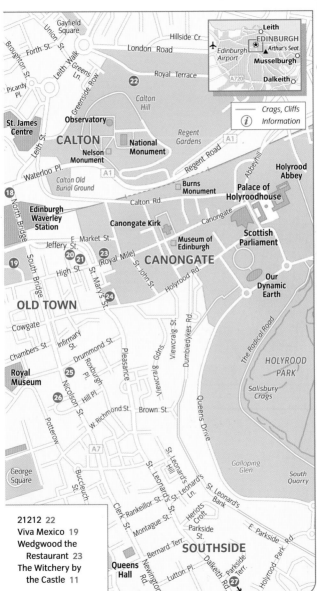

Crags, Cliffs
(i) Information

21212 22
Viva Mexico 19
Wedgwood the
Restaurant 23
The Witchery by
the Castle 11

Leith Dining

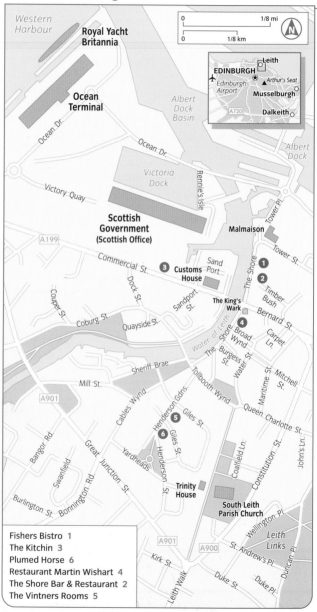

Fishers Bistro 1
The Kitchin 3
Plumed Horse 6
Restaurant Martin Wishart 4
The Shore Bar & Restaurant 2
The Vintners Rooms 5

Dining Best Bets

Best **Vegetarian**
★★ David Bann, *56–58 St. Mary's St. (p 77)*

Best **Hot Chef**
★★★ The Kitchin, *78 Commercial Quay (p 78)*

Most **Romantic**
★ The Vintners Rooms, *The Vaults, 87 Giles St. (p 82)*

Best **Burger**
★ Bell's Diner, *17 St. Stephen St. (p 76)*

Best **Outdoor Dining**
★ Oloroso, *33 Castle St. (p 79)*

Best **Neighborhood Hangout**
★ Sweet Melindas, *11 Roseneath St. (p 81)*

Best **Luxe Afternoon Tea**
Palm Court at the Balmoral Hotel, *Princes St. (p 77)*

Best for **Families**
★ Valvona & Crolla, *19 Elm Row (p 82)*

Best **Cheap Eats**
★ Kebab Mahal, *7 Nicolson Sq. (p 78)*

Best **Innovator**
★★ 21212, *3 Royal Terrace (p 81)*

Best **French Rustic Cooking**
★ La Garrigue, *31 Jeffrey St. (p 79)*

Best **Fresh Fish & Seafood**
★ Fishers Bistro, *1 The Shore (p 77)*

Best **Views**
★★ Forth Floor, *30–34 St. Andrew Sq. (p 78)*

Best **Cafe Diner**
★★ Spoon Café Bistro, *15 Blackfriars St. (p 81)*

Best **Spanish**
★ Barioja, *19 Jeffrey St. (p 76)*

Most **Atmospheric**
★ The Witchery by the Castle, *Castlehill (p 82)*

Best **Extravagance**
★★★ Restaurant Martin Wishart, *54 The Shore (p 80)*

French dining at Vintners Rooms.

Edinburgh Dining A to Z

Laidback tapas bar Barioja.

★ **Barioja** OLD TOWN *SPANISH*
A laidback tapas bar which is fun, friendly, and often lively in the evenings. Portions are substantial and reasonably priced. *19 Jeffrey St. ☎ 0131/557-3622. www.barioja.co. uk. Main courses £6–£15. AE, MC, V. Lunch & dinner daily. Bus: 36. Map p 72.*

★ **Bell's Diner** STOCKBRIDGE *AMERICAN* If you're desperate for a chargrilled patty of real ground

beef, seek out this tiny diner. Burgers are cooked to order with a variety of toppings (from cheese to garlic butter). *17 St. Stephen St. ☎ 0131/225-8116. Main courses £6.50–£9. MC, V. Dinner daily, lunch Sat only. Bus: 24, 29, or 42. Map p 72.*

★ **Café Royal Oyster Bar** NEW TOWN *SEAFOOD/FISH* Much of this 140-year-old cafe-bar's Victorian stained timber and glass is impressively still in place. Mains obviously feature shellfish —but there are meat and vegetarian options available too. *17a W. Register St. ☎ 0131/556-1884. www.caferoyal.org.uk. Main courses £14–£22. AE, MC, V. Lunch & dinner daily. Bus: 8 or 29. Map p 72.*

Café St. Honoré NEW TOWN *FRENCH* This Parisian-style brasserie is French in spirit, but the menu is peppered with references to Scottish ingredients, from Borders beef to Stornoway black pudding (rather than Gallic boudin noir). *34 NW Thistle St. Lane. ☎ 0131/226-2211. www.cafe sthonore.com. Main courses £10–£22. AE, MC, V. Lunch & dinner daily. Bus: 24, 29, or 42. Map p 72.*

Café Royal Oyster Bar.

Two for Tea?

A formal choice for the classically British experience of afternoon tea is The Palm Court in the Balmoral Hotel, 1 Princes St. (☎ 0131/556-2414), where you'll find substantial and filling offerings (and a price of about £25). More casual (and less costly) is **The Edinburgh Larder,** 15 Blackfriars St. (☎ 0131/556-6922). Just off the Royal Mile, it has specially sourced teas and coffees, as well as rich cakes.

★ **Castle Terrace** WEST END MODERN SCOTTISH   New to the city in 2010, this is a spin-off of The Kitchin (see p 78) with Dominic Jack in charge. It shares the Kitchin ethos—'from nature to plate'—with dishes such as herb ravioli with Scottish Crowdie cheese and vanilla creme brulée. The restaurant features a full meat-free menu as well. *33/35 Castle Terrace* ☎ *0131/229-1222. www.castleterracerestaurant. com. Main courses £23–£28; set lunch £12. MC, V. Lunch & dinner Tues–Sat. Bus 1, 10, 15, 16, 24, or 34. Map p 72.*

★★ **David Bann** OLD TOWN VEGE-TARIAN   Chef David Bann has been at the forefront of meat-free cooking in Edinburgh for some time and his meals are modern, inventive, and most importantly tasty. The dining room is as stylish as the cooking. *56–58 St. Mary's St.* ☎ *0131/556-5888. www.davidbann.com. Main courses £7.50–£12. AE, MC, V. Lunch & dinner daily. Bus: 36. Map p 72.*

The Dome Grill Room NEW TOWN INTERNATIONAL   Corinthian columns, intricate mosaic flooring, and towering flower arrangements—all housed under an elaborate domed ceiling. Many people come here for the decor alone. Steaks are specially selected and aged an extra 28 days for tenderness. *14 George St.* ☎ *0131/624-8624.*

www.thedomeedinburgh.com. Main courses £10–£22. AE, DC, MC, V. Lunch & dinner daily. Bus: 45. Map p 72.

★★ **Dusit** NEW TOWN THAI   This unassuming restaurant has the reputation for serving the best fine-dining Thai food in the city. A number of dishes make use of seasonal Scottish produce, such as venison, scallops, or guinea fowl. *49a Thistle St.* ☎ *0131/220-6846. www.dusit. co.uk. Main courses £12–£18. AE, MC, V. Lunch & dinner daily. Bus: 24, 29, or 42. Map p 72.*

Fishers Bistro LEITH FISH   A favorite for seafood, the chefs here

Posh ambiance at the Dome Grill Room.

serve up enticing dishes such as fresh Loch Fyne oysters, crispy fish cakes, and West Coast halibut. Alternatively, there are sirloins and venison. *1 The Shore.* ☎ *0131-554-5666. www.fishersbistros.co.uk Main courses £12–£16. AE, MC, V. Lunch & dinner daily. Bus: 16, 22, 35, or 36. Map p 74.*

★★ **Forth Floor** NEW TOWN *MODERN SCOTTISH* This restaurant/brasserie at the top of the Harvey Nichols department store dishes out excellent contemporary fine dining, whether langoustine bisque or roast monkfish with homemade chorizo. The brasserie menu offers less pricey alternatives. *30–34 St. Andrew Sq.* ☎ *0131/524-8350. www.harvey nichols.com. Main courses £16–£25; set lunch £20. AE, DC, MC, V. Lunch daily & dinner Tues–Sat. Bus: 8, 10, 12, or 45. Map p 72.*

The Grain Store OLD TOWN *MODERN SCOTTISH* In its upstairs dining room, the Grain Store delivers ambitious, innovative cooking, cooking-up delights such as Scottish venison with beetroot fondant, or a medley of sea bass and scallops. *30 Victoria St.* ☎ *0131/225-7635. www. grainstore-restaurant.co.uk. Main courses £17–£25; set lunch £13. AE, MC, V. Lunch & dinner daily. Map p 72.*

kids Henderson's Vegetarian Restaurant NEW TOWN *VEGETARIAN* This is Edinburgh's longtime stalwart of healthy, inexpensive, and totally vegetarian cuisine. Expect to dine on vegetable stroganoff or mushroom and spinach quiche. Wines include some organic options. *94 Hanover St.* ☎ *0131/225-2131. www.hendersonsofedinburgh.co.uk. Main courses £6–£10; set lunch £9.50. MC, V. Breakfast, lunch & dinner Mon–Sat. Bus: 13, 23, or 27. Map p 72.*

Howies OLD TOWN *MODERN SCOTTISH* Of this local chain's four branches, the one near the Royal Mile is most convenient for tourists. After 20 years, Howies' motto remains 'fine food without the faff'—whether honey-cured salmon or gnocchi in pesto. *10–14 Victoria St.* ☎ *0131/225-1721. www.howies. uk.com. Main courses £8–£14. AE, MC, V. Lunch & dinner daily. Bus: 2, 41, or 42. Map p 72.*

★ **Kebab Mahal** SOUTHSIDE *INDIAN* Drawing a cross section of city folk, this basic, inexpensive Indian restaurant—where you may have to share your table with others—is an Edinburgh landmark. No alcohol is served (or allowed inside), but it is open late. *7 Nicolson Sq.* ☎ *0131/667-5214. Main courses £4–£6. Lunch & dinner daily (closed for Fri prayers noon–2pm). No credit cards. Bus: 3, 5, 29, 31, or 35. Map p 72.*

★★★ **The Kitchin** LEITH *MODERN SCOTTISH/FRENCH* Chef Tom Kitchin quickly garnered a Michelin star after opening this restaurant (his first) about 6 years ago. The young, curly-topped chef is becoming a regular on UK TV, and his

A vegetarian dish at Henderson's.

French-inspired recipes use top seasonal Scottish ingredients. *78 Commercial Quay.* ☎ *0131/555-1755. www.thekitchin.com. Main courses £30; set lunch £25. MC, V. Lunch & dinner Tues–Sat. Bus: 16, 22, 35, or 36. Map p 74.*

★ **La Garrigue** OLD TOWN *FRENCH* Its chef and owner hails from southern France, and here he successfully recreates that region's fresh and rustic cooking. The feeling of the dining room is casual but still stylish. *31 Jeffrey St.* ☎ *0131/557-3032. www.lagarrigue.co.uk. Set lunch £14; set dinner £25. AE, MC, V. Lunch & dinner Mon–Sat. Bus: 36. Map p 72.*

★ **Number One** NEW TOWN *MODERN SCOTTISH* The premier restaurant in the city's foremost city-center hotel has a well-earned Michelin star for its superior cuisine. Service is better still. *In the Balmoral Hotel, 1 Princes St.* ☎ *0131/557-6727. www.thebalmoralhotel.com. Set dinner £60. AE, DC, MC, V. Dinner daily. Bus: 3, 8, 19, or 30. Map p 72.*

★ **Oloroso** NEW TOWN *SCOTTISH/ INTERNATIONAL* With the summer veranda and excellent panoramic views, the atmosphere here feels

Imaginative cooking in a swanky setting at Oloroso.

rather swanky. Cuisine is imaginative—for starters, try the breast of wood pigeon with glazed pear, Jerusalem artichoke purée, and juniper jus. *33 Castle St.* ☎ *0131/226-7614. www.oloroso.co.uk. Main courses £15–£25; set lunch £20. MC, V. Lunch & dinner daily. Bus: 24, 29, or 42. Map p 72.*

★ **Ondine** OLD TOWN *SEAFOOD/ FISH* A relative newcomer, this restaurant and chef-owner Roy Brett quickly gained an enviable reputation for cooking brilliant fish dishes

Source to City

Edinburgh has a weekly Farmers Market that rivals any in the country. The market is located at Castle Terrace, with Edinburgh Castle towering above. On the first Saturday of the month, a Slow Food cooking demonstration features some of the best Scottish produce. Many of the producers also have samples to taste for free, while others have cooked food you can take away or eat at outdoor tables nearby. Among the notable stallholders, try to seek out Ballencrieff Rare Pedigree Pigs, Arran Cheese, Carmichael Estate Farm Meats, Bellfield Organic Fruit and Vegetables, Stoat's Porridge Bar, and Madame Bouvy's Tartes. The market runs year round every Saturday from 9am to 2pm. ☎ 0131/652-5940. www.edinburgh farmersmarket.co.uk. *Bus 1, 10, 15, 16, 24, or 34.*

Delicately served, seasonal food at Martin Wishart.

using ingredients from sustainable sources. The shellfish platter is highly recommended. *2 George IV Bridge.* ☎ *0131/226-1888. www. ondinerestaurant.co.uk. Main courses £12–£34; set lunch £17. MC, V. Lunch daily, dinner Mon–Sat. Bus: 23, 27, 42, or 67. Map p 72.*

★ **Plumed Horse** LEITH *FRENCH/ MODERN BRITISH* This traditional eatery is considered among the top dining destinations in greater Edinburgh. Feast on rose of veal with Madeira cream or monkfish on garlic-infused mash potatoes. *50–54 Henderson St.* ☎ *0131/554-5556. www.plumedhorse.co.uk. Set lunch £26; set dinner £55. MC, V. Lunch & dinner Tues–Sat. Bus: 22, 35, or 36. Map p 74.*

★ **Redwood** STOCKBRIDGE *AMERI-CAN* California cuisine remains a bit of a novelty here, but Golden State chef Annette Sprague effectively mixes the influences of Japan, Mexico, and more in her menu. *33a St. Stephen St.* ☎ *0131/225-8342. www.redwood-restaurant.co.uk. Set dinner £24. MC, V. Dinner Wed–Sat. Bus: 24, 29, or 42. Map p 72.*

★★★ **Restaurant Martin Wishart** LEITH *MODERN FRENCH* One of Scotland's leading chefs, Wishart takes the accumulating accolades in his stride and constantly strives to improve the quality of this high-priced establishment where the menu is seasonal and the wine list superb. If it's an option, try the John Dory with leeks, salsify, mussel, and almond gratin. *54 The Shore.* ☎ *0131/553-3557. www.martin-wishart.co.uk. Main courses £20–£35; set lunch £25; set gourmet dinner £70. AE, MC, V. Lunch & dinner Tues–Sat. Bus: 22 or 36. Map p 74.*

Rhubarb SOUTHSIDE *MODERN SCOTTISH* Housed in 17th-century Prestonfield House, this posh, theatrical restaurant offers a sense of drama

King o' the Puddin' Race

Haggis, the much-misunderstood traditional dish of Scotland, can be an acquired taste, but it's honestly tasty. **Macsween of Edinburgh** (www.macsween.co.uk) is a long-established family business specializing in what poet Robert Burns lionized as the 'King o' the Puddin' Race'. Their version includes lamb, beef, oatmeal, onions, and various seasonings and spices—all cooked together in a natural casing. You can buy it at many supermarkets and food stores in Edinburgh. They also make a popular vegetarian version.

and flair. The menu is a bit fancy as well, with dishes such as hand-dived scallops, Iberico de Bellota jamon, and quince. *Priestfield Rd.* ☎ *0131/225-1333. www.prestonfield.com. Main courses £18–£25; set lunch £17. AE, DC, MC, V. Lunch & dinner daily. Bus: 2, 14, or 30. Map p 72.*

Santini Ristorante WEST END *ITALIAN* This modern restaurant, set in a building adjacent to the Sheraton Grand Hotel, serves some of the capital's classiest Italian cooking. *8 Conference St.* ☎ *0131/221-7788. Main courses £15–£22; set lunch £10. AE, MC, V. Lunch & dinner Mon–Fri, dinner Sat. Bus: 1, 2, 10, 24, or 34. Map p 72.*

Seadogs NEW TOWN FISH Come here for traditional fish 'n' chips and big portions of paella (or fish pie) for sharing, or try one of the more innovative dishes like the smoked mackerel with rhubarb jam. *43 Rose St.* ☎ *0131/225-8028. www.seadogsonline.co.uk. Main courses £5–£11. MC, V. Lunch & dinner daily. Bus: 10, 12, 16, 23, or 45. Map p 72.*

★ The Shore Bar & Restaurant LEITH *FISH* Whether eating in the unassuming pub (see p 91) or the slightly more formal dining room, you'll appreciate the simplicity and ease of this operation, dedicated to fresh fish and seafood. *3/4 The Shore.* ☎ *0131/553-5080. Main courses*

Go to The Shore for the freshest seafood.

£10–£16. AE, MC, V. Lunch & dinner daily. Bus: 16, 22, 35, or 36. Map p 74.

★★ kids Spoon Café Bistro OLD TOWN *CAFE* In addition to reasonably-priced snacks and cakes available in the daytime, Spoon's comforting evening menu includes navarin of lamb with seasonal vegetables and puy lentil curry. *6a Nicolson St.* ☎ *0131/557-4567. www.spooncafe.co.uk. Main courses £9–£17. MC, V. Lunch & dinner Mon–Sat. Bus: 3, 5, 29, 31, or 35. Map p 72.*

★ Sweet Melindas SOUTHSIDE *SCOTTISH/FISH* Near the Meadows, this neighborhood favorite merits visits from anyone admiring simple and amiable surroundings. The menu emphasizes fish, which the chefs purchase from the shop next door. *11 Roseneath St.* ☎ *0131/229-7953. Set lunch £12.50; set dinner £22.50. AE, MC, V. Lunch & dinner Tues–Sat, dinner Mon. Bus: 24 or 41. Map p 72.*

★★ 21212 NEW TOWN *MODERN FRENCH* This restaurant has made the biggest splash in the past few years. The five-course dinners are exceptional with odd but compelling combinations of ingredients, such as beef with lemon curd. *3 Royal Terrace.* ☎ *0845/22 21212. Set lunch £25; set dinner £65. AE, MC, V. Lunch & dinner Tues–Sat. Bus: 1, 15, 19, 26, or 34. Map p 72.*

Dramatic dining, both on and off your plate at Rhubarb.

Family-Friendly Fare

If you're looking for a friendly lunch spot, families can't go wrong heading to the Baked Potato Shop, 56 Cockburn St. (☎ 0131/225-7572), just off the High Street in Old Town. Kids can order fluffy baked potatoes with a choice of half a dozen hot fillings. Alternatively, **Valvona & Crolla,** 19 Elm Row (☎ 0131/556-6066), is best known as one of the UK's finest delis, but the cafe in the back handles children in a way that bambini-loving Italians do best.

★ **The Vintners Rooms** LEITH
FRENCH   Housed in a 17th-century French wine store, this romantic restaurant's reputation is secure. Scottish produce is used in a host of confidently inventive Gallic dishes. *The Vaults, 87 Giles St. ☎ 0131/554-6767. www.thevintnersrooms.com. Main courses £18–£23. AE, MC, V. Lunch & dinner Tues–Sat. Bus: 22 or 36. Map p 74.*

Viva Mexico OLD TOWN *MEXICAN*   Mexican cooking is not a particular strength in Edinburgh's cosmopolitan restaurant scene, but this place makes a good go of it. Simple fare is washed down with bottles of cold *cerveza* in a convenient location only seconds from the Royal Mile. *41 Cockburn St. ☎ 0131/226-5145. www.viva-mexico.co.uk. Main courses £8–£15; set lunch £8, MC, V. Bus: 35. Map p 72.*

★ **Wedgwood the Restaurant**
OLD TOWN *MODERN SCOTTISH*

The menu here changes with the seasons and the cooking of chef and owner Paul Wedgwood is always innovative. Try towers of venison in olive and carrot purée and haggis bonbons. *267 Canongate ☎ 0131/558-8737. www.wedgwoodthe restaurant.co.uk. Main courses £15–£24; set lunch £10. MC, V. Lunch & dinner daily. Bus: 36. Map p 72.*

★ **The Witchery by the Castle**
OLD TOWN *SCOTTISH/MODERN BRITISH*   In a historic building that's associated with nearby medieval sites of execution (and a ghost or two), you can expect classy Scottish food in even classier surroundings. Ideal for late sit-down meals (last orders 11:30pm). *Castlehill, Royal Mile. ☎ 0131/225-5613. www.the witchery.com. Main courses £18–£25; set lunch £14. AE, DC, MC, V. Lunch & dinner daily. Bus: 28. Map p 72.* ●

Head to the Witchery By the Castle for well-constructed dishes served in classy surroundings.

Edinburgh Nightlife

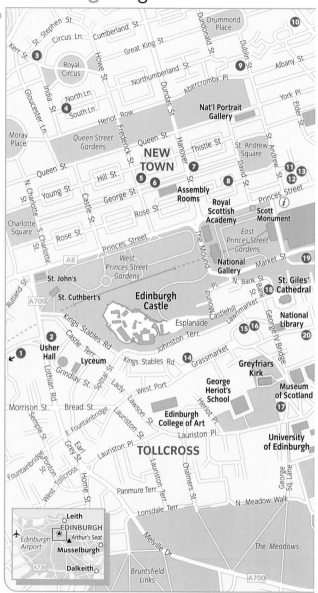

St. Stephen St.
Kerr St.
Circus Ln.
Cumberland St.
Drummond Place ⑩
Royal Circus
Great King St.
Howe St.
Dundonald St.
Dublin St.
Albany St.
⑨
Gloucester Ln.
India St.
North Ln.
④
South Ln.
Heriot Row
Northumberland St.
Abercromby Pl.
York Pl.
Elder St.
Moray Place
Queen Street Gardens
Frederick St.
Dundas St.
Queen St.
Thistle St.
Nat'l Portrait Gallery
St. Andrew Square
NEW TOWN
Hanover St.
⑤ ⑥
⑦
St. Andrew St.
⑪ ⑬
⑫
Queen St.
Hill St.
Young St.
George St.
Rose St.
David St.
Assembly Rooms
⑧
Princes Street
ⓘ
Scott Monument
N. Charlotte St.
Castle St.
Charlotte Square
S. Charlotte St.
Rose St.
Princes Street
Royal Scottish Academy
East Princes Street Gardens
A8
West Princes Street Gardens
The Mound
National Gallery
Market St.
⑲
Ruland St.
A700
St. John's
St. Cuthbert's
Edinburgh Castle
Pl.
N. Bank St.
Bank St.
St. Giles' Cathedral
⑱
Usher Hall
②
①
Castle Terr.
Kings Stables Rd.
Esplanade
Castlehill
Lawnmarket
George IV Bridge
National Library
⑳
Lothian Rd.
Grindlay St.
Spittal St.
Lady Lawson St.
Lyceum
Johnston Terr.
Kings Stables Rd.
⑭
Grassmarket
⑮ ⑯
Greyfriars Kirk
Morrison St.
Bread St.
West Port
George Heriot's School
Heriot Pl.
Museum of Scotland
⑰
E. Fountainbridge
Earl Grey St.
Lauriston St.
Edinburgh College of Art
Lauriston Pl.
Fountainbridge
Ponton St.
Semple St.
West-Tollcross
Home St.
Lauriston Pl.
TOLLCROSS
Chalmers St.
University of Edinburgh
George Sq. Lane
Panmure Terr.
Lauriston Terr.
Lonsdale Terr.
N. Meadow Walk
Melville Dr.
The Meadows
A700
Bruntsfield Links
Leith
✈ EDINBURGH
Edinburgh Airport
★ Arthur's Seat
Musselburgh
A720
Dalkeith ○

Previous Page: Sandy Bell's

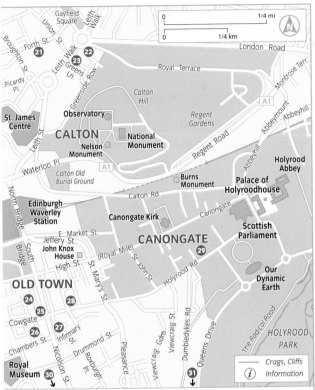

The Abbotsford 8
All Bar One 7
The Bailie Bar 3
The Beehive Inn 14
Black Bo's 28
The Blue Moon Café 10
Bongo Club 29
Bow Bar 15
BrewDog 20
Cabaret Voltaire 24
Café Royal Circle Bar 11
C. C. Bloom's 23
Corn Exchange 1
Deacon Brodie's
  Tavern 18
Ecco Vino 19

Guildford Arms 13
HMV Picturehouse 2
The Jazz Bar 26
Kay's Bar 4
The Liquid Room 16
The Newtown Bar 9
Opal Lounge 6
The Outhouse 21
The Pear Tree House 30
Planet Out 22
Po Na Na 5
The Royal Oak 27
Sandy Bell's 17
The Sheep Heid Inn 31
The Voodoo Rooms 12
Whistlebinkies 25

Leith Nightlife

Boda Bar 6
Bond No. 9 2
The King's
Wark 3
The Pond Bar 4
The Shore 1
Sofi's Bar 5
Victoria 6

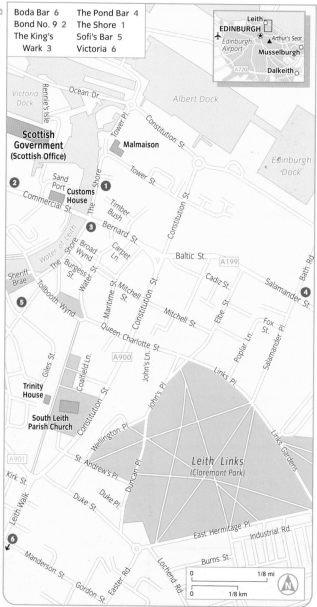

Nightlife Best Bets

Best for Real Ale
★ Bow Bar, *80 West Bow (p 88)*

Best Grassmarket Pub
The Beehive Inn, *18–20
Grassmarket (p 88)*

Best Victorian Bar
★★ Café Royal Circle Bar, *17 W.
Register St. (p 89)*

Best Beer Garden
★ The Outhouse, *12a Broughton St.
Lane (p 90)*

Best Style Bar
Opal Lounge, *51a George St. (p 90)*

Best for Bottled European
Lager
★★ The Pond Bar, *2–4 Bath Rd.
(p 90)*

Best Traditional Pub
★ Guildford Arms, *1–5 W. Register
St. (p 89)*

Best Leith Pub
★★★ The Shore, *3–4 The Shore.
(p 91)*

Best Scottish Folk Hangout
★ Sandy Bell's, *25 Forrest Rd.
(p 92)*

Best Jazz Joint
★ The Jazz Bar, *1a Chambers St.
(p 93)*

Best Rock Club
★ The Liquid Room, *9c Victoria St.
(p 93)*

Best Gay Bar
Planet Out, *6 Baxters Place (p 92)*

Best Dive Bar
★★ Black Bo's, *57 Blackfriars St.
(p 88)*

Best Neighborhood Hangout
★★ The Bailie Bar, *2 St. Stephen St.
(p 88)*

Best Rose Street Pub
★ The Abbotsford, *3 Rose St.
(p 88)*

Best Cabaret
Cabaret Voltaire *36–38 Blair St.
(p 91)*

Live Scottish folk at Sandy Bell's.

Edinburgh Nightlife A to Z

Bars & Pubs

★ The Abbotsford NEW TOWN
Bartenders have been pouring pints here since the early 1900s, and the gaslight era is preserved thanks to dark paneling and an ornate plaster ceiling. The ales on tap change about once a week. *3 Rose St.* ☎ *0131/225-5276. Bus: 3, 28, or 45. Map p 84.*

All Bar One NEW TOWN   All Bar One is a well-run chain with modern decor and a decent selection of wines by the glass. Drop by after 5pm Sun–Wed for cheaper cocktails and dine on global tapas or a selection of mains until 9 or 10pm daily. *29 George St.* ☎ *0131/226-9971. Bus: 24, 28, or 45. Map p 84.*

★★ The Bailie Bar STOCKBRIDGE
This traditional pub in the heart of Stockbridge could possibly serve as the unofficial public meeting hall for the neighborhood. Often there's plenty of banter between the locals and staff in the basement bar, which normally has at least three real ales on tap. *2 St. Stephen St.* ☎ *0131/225-4673. Bus: 24, 29, or 42. Map p 84.*

The Beehive Inn OLD TOWN
You have plenty of choice when it comes to finding a pub on Grassmarket, but this inn offers lots of seating over three different rooms and doesn't try to flog any dodgy historic connections. There's a beer garden at the back and streetside seating for good weather. *18–20 Grassmarket.* ☎ *0131/225-7171. Bus: 2. Map p 84.*

★★ Black Bo's OLD TOWN   This bar is slightly unconventional and one of Frommer's favorites. It is neither a traditional pub nor a particularly stylish place, but it does have an easy air of hipness and cordiality. *57 Blackfriars St.* ☎ *0131/557-6136. Bus: 35. Map p 84.*

★ Boda Bar LEITH   The first 'Swedish' bar in Edinburgh and older sibling to Sofi (p 91), Boda proved that sensitive owners could revamp a traditional pub but not drain it of personality. Casual, shabby chic, and welcoming. *229 Leith Walk* ☎ *0131/553-5900. www.bodabar.com. Bus: 10, 12, 14, 16, 22, or 49. Map p 86.*

Bond No. 9 LEITH   If you desire a proper Manhattan on the rocks or desert-dry Martini in Leith, come to this lounge bar in a former whisky bond. The comforting, seasonal gastro pub food is also worth a try. *84 Commercial St.* ☎ *0131/555-5578. www.bondno9.co.uk. Bus: 16, 22, 35, or 36. Map p 86.*

★ Bow Bar OLD TOWN   It feels like a classic time-honored Edinburgh pub, but is actually only around 20 years old. Still, it looks the part, featuring excellent cask-conditioned ales and a superior whisky selection. Good for a quiet drink off the Royal Mile. *80 West*

Sample a whisky at Bow Bar.

The Guildford Arms.

Bow. ☎ 0131/226-7667. *Bus: 2 or 35. Map p 84.*

BrewDog Edinburgh OLD TOWN BrewDog is a brand of innovative beers made in northeast Scotland and this is the company's second branch of bars (after Aberdeen) featuring their very own brews on tap: from Trashy Blonde to Punk IPA. *143–145 Cowgate. No phone. www. brewdog.com. Bus: 7, 31, 37, or 47. Map p 84.*

★★ **Café Royal Circle Bar** NEW TOWN The high Victorian design of Café Royal was nearly demolished in the late 1960s, but thank goodness the wrecking ball wasn't used. Spacious booths and plenty of room around the bar combine to make this one of the most comfortable places to drink in the city. *17 W. Register St.* ☎ *0131/556-1884. www.caferoyal.org.uk. Bus: 8 or 17. Map p 84.*

Deacon Brodie's Tavern OLD TOWN This Royal Mile pub is primarily populated by tourists and local lawyers. Its name, of course, perpetuates the memory of William

Brodie (1741–88), a good citizen by day and nasty robber by night (and the inspiration behind Dr. Jekyll and Mr. Hyde). *435 Lawnmarket.* ☎ *0131/ 225-6531. Bus: 35. Map p 84.*

Ecco Vino As the name suggests, this Enoteca-style bar offers more than 20 wines by the glass and several more if you wish to share a bottle. Food focuses on authentic Italian fare from antipasti to simple pasta dishes. *19 Cockburn St.* ☎ *0131/225-1441. www.ecco vinoedinburgh.com. Bus: 36. Map p 84.*

★ **Guildford Arms** NEW TOWN From the revolving doors to the arched windows with etched glass, the Guildford Arms has old-school styling and a bustling atmosphere to match. This is a landmark real ale pub with plenty of hand-pulled beers available. *1–5 W. Register St.* ☎ *0131/556-4312. www.guildford arms.com. Bus: 8 or 17. Map p 84.*

Kay's Bar NEW TOWN If you want the feel of a real, honest-to-goodness traditional Edinburgh bar, then this fits the bill. Housed in a one-time wine merchant's on a quiet New Town lane, the pub's one nod to modernity is the big screen TV—although cribbage proves equally popular here. *39 Jamaica St.* ☎ *0131/ 225-1858. Bus: 24, 29, or 42. Map p 84.*

The King's Wark LEITH In historic premises, the King's Wark is a traditional pub which offers up pretty decent pub grub—tuck into mussels in chili white wine sauce or whole plaice with shrimp butter. At the weekend you can get a cooked breakfast, but you may need to make a reservation. *36 The Shore.* ☎ *0131/554-9260. www.thekings wark.co.uk. Bus: 22, 35, or 36. Map p. 86.*

Opal Lounge NEW TOWN If you want to experience a so-called urban 'style bar' (that is uber-modern and usually featuring DJs) then this is where you should head to. The Opal draws a predominantly young, well-dressed, and affluent crowd, including, in the past, Prince William and Kate (the Duke and Duchess of Cambridge). *51a George St.* ☎ *0131/226-2275. www.opal lounge.co.uk. Bus: 24, 29, or 42. Map p 84.*

★ The Outhouse NEW TOWN Down a cobbled lane off Broughton Street, this modern bar has a secluded if popular beer garden (equipped with outdoor heaters) out back. The selection of international bottled beers, from Asahi Dry to Erdinger Weiss is excellent. *12a Broughton St. Lane.* ☎ *0131/557-6688. Bus: 8 or 17. Map p 84.*

The Pear Tree House SOUTH-SIDE The large beer garden is typically packed here during the Edinburgh Festival and just about any dry day during the local college's term time. Ideal for a pint and soaking up the sun. There's usually a barbeque over the summer months too. *34 West Nicolson St.* ☎ *0131/667-7533. Bus: 41, 42, or 67. Map p 84.*

★★ The Pond Bar LEITH As bohemian as Black Bo's (p 88), the decor of this bar is eclectic to say the least. The highlights of the drinks selection are draft and bottled European lagers, especially German, Belgian, and Polish brews, and two types of Czech Krusovice on draught. *2–4 Bath Rd. at Salamander St.* ☎ *0131/467-3825. Bus: 12. Map p 86.*

The Sheep Heid Inn SOUTHSIDE The adjacent village of Duddingston is just below Arthur's Seat and this historic pub (est. 1360) has been serving locals for as long as any bar in the entire country. Various real

Late Night Snacks

It is late and you're famished, where do you go? The area around Edinburgh University is the one place to check for kebabs. On Rose Street South Lane, however, in New Town, **Turkish Kitchen** is the best option. Open till 3am at the weekend, the menu has meze style platters and proper main courses such as *tavuk iskender* with marinated chicken, garlic, and yogurt. 120–122 Rose Street South Lane ☎ 0131/226-2212. www.turkishkitchen edinburgh.co.uk. Bus 10, 11, 12, 16, 22, 24, or 25.

Late Nights During the Festival

During the festival season in Edinburgh, from late July right through to the beginning of September, you can expect most bars and pubs to keep later hours. Most apply for temporary licenses to extend opening until 1am to 3am, when they might ordinarily close at midnight.

ale and cider festivals are held over the summer months. There's also an old fashioned skittles alley inside the pub and a beer garden. *43–45 The Causeway, Duddingston.* ☎ *0131/661-7974. www.sheepheid.co.uk. Bus: 42. Map p 84.*

★★★ **The Shore** LEITH Best of the best, this pub fits seamlessly into Leith's seaside port ambience, without the usual cork and netting decorations. On 3 nights of the week, people gather here for live folk and jazz music. *3–4 The Shore.* ☎ *0131/553-5080. www.theshore. biz. Bus: 16 or 36. Map p 86.*

★★ **Sofi's Bar** LEITH Owned by the same Swedish folk as Boda Bar (p 88), this place is cool without trying too hard. There are several theme nights every week aimed at everyone from film lovers to knitters, and a decent selection of wine and cocktails. *65 Henderson St.* ☎ *0131/555-7019. www.bodabar. com. Bus: 22, 35, or 36. Map p. 86.*

Dance Clubs
Bongo Club OLD TOWN Offering a varied program of music throughout the week—funk, dub, and experimental—this venue has more reasonably priced drinks than many. *Moray House, 37 Holyrood Rd.* ☎ *0131/558-7604. www.thebongo club.co.uk. Up to £10 cover. Bus: 35. Map p 84.*

Cabaret Voltaire OLD TOWN This club's music mix includes house, indie, and techno—plus there's a program of gigs spread over the month. *36–38 Blair St.* ☎ *0131/220-6176. www.thecabaret voltaire.com. Up to £12 cover. Bus: 35. Map p 84.*

★ **The Liquid Room** OLD TOWN This busy but smallish venue is a club when not hosting rock groups (see p 93). Saturday-night clubs differ weekly, covering everything from indie gatherings to techno dance sessions. *9c Victoria St.* ☎ *0131/225-2564. www.liquid room.com. Cover: £10. Map p 84.*

Po Na Na NEW TOWN This is the Edinburgh branch of a successful chain of clubs in Britain with a Moroccan Kasbah theme. The dance mix is hip-hop and funk, or disco and the sounds of the '80s. *43b Frederick St.* ☎ *0131/226-2224. www.ponana.co.uk. Up to £8 cover. Bus: 80. Map p 84.*

Folk Music
The Royal Oak SOUTHSIDE This split-level pub, often open until 2am, is the home of live Scottish folk music. Local musicians can be heard every night of the week and on Sundays from 8:30pm various guests appear at the 'Wee Folk Club'. *1 Infirmary St.* ☎ *0131/557-2976.*

The Voodoo Rooms.

www.royal-oak-folk.com. £3 cover Sun. Bus: 3, 5, 8, or 29. Map p 84.

★ **Sandy Bell's** OLD TOWN   This small, corner pub near the Museum of Scotland is a landmark for Scottish and Gaelic culture, with live acts nearly every night and all day Saturday. *25 Forrest Rd. ☎ 0131/225-2751. No cover. Bus: 2 or 42. Map p 84.*

Gay, Lesbian & Transgender

The Blue Moon Café NEW TOWN   This modest establishment is among the oldest gay cafes in the UK. Located in the heart of the city's gay scene, it serves hearty, basic fare upstairs, whilst downstairs in the basement, the relaxed, low-key Deep Blue Bar is open daily for drinks. *36 Broughton St. ☎ 0131/556-2788. www.bluemooncafe.co.uk. Bus: 8. Map p 84.*

C. C. Bloom's NEW TOWN   The heart of the gay community is an area below Calton Hill, incorporating the top of Leith Walk around the Playhouse Theatre and nearby

Broughton Street. This bar (named after Bette Midler's character in Beaches) is a longtime stalwart in the scene. *23–24 Greenside Pl. ☎ 0131/556-9331. Bus: 1, 5, 7, 22, 25, 33, or 49. Map p 84.*

The Newtown Bar NEW TOWN   Slightly off the beaten track, tucked down a lane, this bar has been refurbished recently. Mainly popular with men, it has a contemporary feel and includes an outdoor beer garden. *26b Dublin St. ☎ 0131/538-7775. Bus: 10, 12, 15, 26, or 44. Map p 84.*

Planet Out NEW TOWN   This venue is another of Edinburgh's long-running and enduringly popular gay nightspots. Just down the hill from C. C. Bloom's, with a young clubby crowd, it draws a slightly higher percentage of lesbians than most of its nearby competitors. *6 Baxters Pl. ☎ 0131/524-0061. Bus: 1, 5, 7, 22, 25, 33, or 49. Map p 84.*

Victoria NEW TOWN   Not strictly GLBT but certainly gay-friendly with a mixed clientele. You can have a say in the entertainment offered, too, at the BYOF (bring your own food) events. There are about 50 different European beers and lagers in bottles and on draught. *265 Leith Walk* ☎ *0131/555-1638. Bus: 14, 29, 31, 37, or 49. Map p 86.*

Rock & Jazz

Corn Exchange SLATEFORD A bit of a haul from the city center, this 3,000 capacity hall books rock and pop performers from Radiohead to Adele. *11 New Market Rd.* ☎ *0131/477-3500. www.ece. uk.com. Ticket prices vary. Bus: 4 or 28. Suburban train: Slateford. Map p 84.*

HMV Picture House WEST END A popular and reasonably new addition to the live music scene, though it has frequent club nights too, such as the twisted pop and alternative rhythms of Beat Control at the weekend. *31 Lothian Rd.* ☎ *0131/ 221-2280. www.edinburgh-picture house.co.uk. Ticket prices vary. Bus: 1, 22, 30, or 34. Map p 84.*

★ **The Jazz Bar** OLD TOWN This basement bar is owned by a practicing jazz drummer, who occasionally sits in with performers (a few of them internationally renowned). The only purpose-built space dedicated to jazz in the city. *1a Chambers St.* ☎ *0131/220-4298. www.thejazzbar.co.uk. Cover £3–£10. Bus: 3, 5, 8, or 29. Map p 84.*

★ **The Liquid Room** OLD TOWN With space for fewer than 1,000, this is Edinburgh's best venue for seeing the sweat off the brows of bands, whether the reunion tour of the Alarm or Half Man Half Biscuit. *9c Victoria St.* ☎ *0131/225-2564. www.liquidroom.com. Ticket prices vary. Bus: 23, 27, 41, or 45. Map p 84.*

The Voodoo Rooms NEW TOWN Once a part of the Café Royal on the ground floor (p 89), the owners spruced up the historical premises in 2008 and turned it into a destination for live music as well as club nights. *19a West Register St.* ☎ *0131/556-7060. www.thevoodoo rooms.com. Ticket prices vary. Bus: 1, 8, 19, or 34. Map p 84.*

Whisky: The Water of Life

When you're in Scotland, you don't need to ask for a Scotch whisky. Everyone here just calls it whisky. Connoisseurs prefer varieties of *single malt* whisky rather than blended versions such as Johnnie Walker, Dewar's, or Bells. The flavors and aromas of single malt whiskies depend largely on where they are distilled: Those from the Hebridean Islands, such as Talisker on Skye or Ardbeg on Islay, are best known for their strong, peaty, and slightly briny flavors. Those from the Highlands, say the lovely Glenmorangie, are less smoky and a bit sweeter. My all-time favorite would probably be Highland Park from the far reaches of Orkney: well-balanced and very drinkable. Add a few drops of tap water to your dram; it helps lift the aromas and flavors.

Burlesque Edinburgh

Burlesque and cabaret acts have been involved in a stunning revival in recent years in the UK. The glamorous **Club Noir** (www.clubnoir.co.uk), though based predominantly in Glasgow, often comes to the capital's **HMV Picture House** (p 93). **The Caves** (8-12 Niddry Street South ☎ 0131/557-8989) is another location for fetish events, such as Torture Garden with its kinky brand of cabaret. One Friday a month, **Confusion is Sex** takes over the Bongo Club (p 91). Orchestrated by the not easily intimidated Gamma Ray Dali, it mixes electro, burlesque, live bands, and pole dancing. You can even take a class in burlesque for beginners at the **Dancebase** on the Grassmarket, www.dancebase.co.uk.

Whistlebinkies OLD TOWN This stone vaulted bar just off the Cowgate regularly has live music, predominantly featuring local acts. It is said that KT Tunstall cut her performing teeth here. Sometimes up to six bands a night play. *4-6 South Bridge.* ☎ *0131/557-5114. www.whistlebinkies.com. Free entry Sun–Thurs; before midnight Fri and Sat. Bus: 7, 31, 37, or 47. Map p 84.* ●

Edinburgh **A&E**

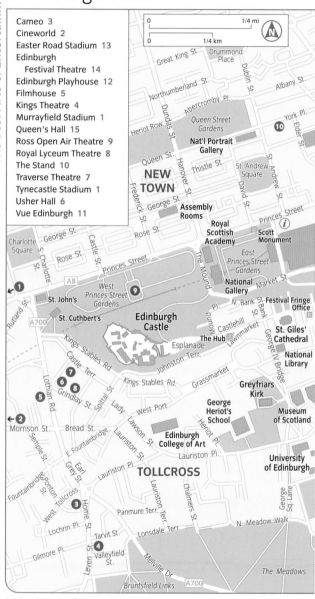

Cameo 3
Cineworld 2
Easter Road Stadium 13
Edinburgh
  Festival Theatre 14
Edinburgh Playhouse 12
Filmhouse 5
Kings Theatre 4
Murrayfield Stadium 1
Queen's Hall 15
Ross Open Air Theatre 9
Royal Lyceum Theatre 8
The Stand 10
Traverse Theatre 7
Tynecastle Stadium 1
Usher Hall 6
Vue Edinburgh 11

Previous Page: Royal Lyceum Theatre.

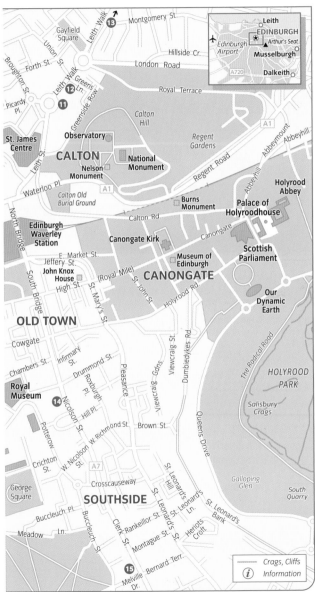

Arts & Entertainment Best Bets

The Stand comedy club.

Best **Comedy Club**
★★ The Stand, *5 York Place (p 99)*

Best **Art House Cinema**
★★★ Filmhouse, *88 Lothian Rd.*
(p 99)

Best **Concert Hall**
★★★ Usher Hall, *71 Lothian Rd.*
(p 100)

Best for **Contemporary Drama**
★★★ Traverse Theatre, *10*
Cambridge St. (p 101)

Best for **Shakespeare**
★★ Royal Lyceum Theatre,
Grindlay St. (p 100)

Best for **Family Entertainment**
★ Edinburgh Playhouse, *18–22*
Greenside Place (p 100)

Best for **Ballet**
Edinburgh Festival Theatre, *13–29*
Nicolson St. (p 99)

Best **Victorian Theater**
★ Kings Theatre, *2 Leven St. (p 100)*

Best **Open Air Performance
Space**
Ross Open Air Theatre, *W. Princes
Street Gardens (p 100)*

Best **Festival**
Edinburgh Festival Fringe, *(p 101)*

Best **Sports Spectacle**
Six Nations Rugby, *Murrayfield
Stadium (p 101)*

Best **Place to Hear Authors**
Edinburgh International Book
Festival, *Charlotte Sq. (p 102)*

Best **Small Concert Hall**
★ Queen's Hall, *Clerk St. (p 99)*

Best **Street Party**
Edinburgh's Hogmanay, *Princes St.
(p 100)*

Arts & Entertainment A to Z

Ballet & Opera
Edinburgh Festival Theatre
SOUTHSIDE This 1,915-seat venue dates to the 1920s, though a theater has stood on this site since 1830. It was completely renovated prior to the 1994 Edinburgh Festival (hence its name). The venue hosts opera and dance, as well as a wide scope of entertainment, which can include anything from comedian John Cleese to the Shaolin Warriors. *13–29 Nicolson St. ☎ 0131/529-6000. www.fctt.org.uk. Ticket prices vary. Bus: 2, 3, 5, 7, 8, 14, 21, 29, 31, 33, 37, 42, or 49. Map p 96.*

Cinema
★ **Cameo** WEST END This superb art house is occasionally threatened with redevelopment but it remains one of the best independent film houses in Scotland, showing arts, indie, foreign, and classic cinema. *38 Home St. ☎ 0871-704-2052. www.picturehouses.co.uk. Tickets £4.80–£7.30. Bus: 1, 10, 15, 17, 24, 28, 35, or 45. Map p 96.*

Cineworld WEST END A branch of a chain of multiplex cinemas across the UK. It combines big

Cameo café in the superb Independent filmhouse.

releases and Hollywood blockbusters with art house and some foreign films as well. *Fountain Park, 130 Dundee St. ☎ 0871/200-2000. www.cineworld.co.uk. Tickets £6.50–£10. Bus: 34 or 38. Map p 96.*

★★★ **Filmhouse** WEST END A must stop for any visiting film buffs, this is Edinburgh's most important movie house. The three screens show mainly world cinema, art house, and independent films, including documentaries and shorts. The Filmhouse also hosts discussions and lectures with directors. *88 Lothian Rd. ☎ 0131/228-2688. www.filmhousecinema.com. Tickets £2.60–£5.60. Bus: 1, 10, 11, 15, 16, 17, 24, or 34. Map p 96.*

Vue Edinburgh NEW TOWN This big glass-fronted multiplex below Calton Hill presents mainstream commercial releases. *Omni Centre. Greenside Place (at top of Leith Walk). ☎ 0871/224-0240. www.myvue.com. Tickets £4.50–£8. Bus: 7 or 22. Map p 96.*

Comedy
★★ **The Stand** NEW TOWN Just down the hill from St. Andrew Square, this is the premier, local venue for stand-up comedy. Big acts are reserved for weekends, while local talent takes the stage during the week. *5 York Place (near Queen St.). ☎ 0131/558-7272. www.the stand.co.uk. Tickets £1.50–£10. Bus: 8 or 17. Map p 96.*

Concert Halls
★ **Queen's Hall** SOUTHSIDE About a mile south of Old Town, the Queen's Hall began life as the Hope Park Chapel, but was upgraded in the 1970s (coinciding with Queen Elizabeth's silver jubilee) to accommodate concerts. It's primarily a

For Auld Lang Syne, my Dear . . .

Hogmanay, or New Year's Eve, is traditionally a bigger event than Christmas for the Scots. Edinburgh annually hosts one of the grandest parties on the planet, and the celebrations can begin a few days in advance with street parties and big bonfires. On New Year's Eve rock bands play in Princes Street Gardens and fireworks fill the skies, launched from most of the city's hills. For information, visit **www.edinburghs hogmanay.com**.

Hogmanay fireworks.

venue for classical works, though eclectic bands such the Drive by Truckers or The Unthanks perform here, too. *Clerk St. (at Hope Park Terrace).* ☎ *0131/668-2019. www. thequeenshall.net. Ticket prices vary. Bus: 5, 7, 8, or 29. Map p 96.*

Ross Open Air Theatre NEW TOWN   This bandstand on the western end of Princes Street Gardens, in the shadow of Edinburgh Castle, is open during the summer for outdoor concerts. The space particularly comes alive during festivals. *W. Princes Street Gardens.* ☎ *0131/220-4351. Ticket prices vary. Bus: 3, 4, or 25. Map p 96.*

★★★ Usher Hall WEST END This Beaux Arts building, opened in 1914, is equivalent to Carnegie Hall. During the annual Edinburgh Festival, the 2,900-seat auditorium hosts orchestras such as the London Philharmonic. But it's not only for classical music—top touring jazz, world music, and pop acts play here, too. *71 Lothian Rd. (at Cambridge St.).* ☎ *0131/228-1155. www. usherhall.co.uk. Ticket prices vary. Bus: 1, 10, 11, 15, 16, 17, 24, or 34. Map p 96.*

Drama
★ Edinburgh Playhouse NEW TOWN   One of the largest UK theaters (with more than 3,000 seats), this is the venue for popular plays and touring West End musicals, such as the Lion King. *18–22 Greenside Place (top of Leith Walk).* ☎ *0131/524-3333. www.edinburgh-playhouse.co.uk. Ticket prices vary. Bus: 5 or 22. Map p 96.*

★ Kings Theatre TOLLCROSS This late Victorian venue, with an impressive domed ceiling and red-brick frontage, offers a wide repertoire including productions by the Scottish National Theatre as well as modern dance and opera. *2 Leven St.* ☎ *0131/529-6000. www.fctt.org.uk. Ticket prices vary. Bus: 1, 10, 15, 17, 24, 28, 35, or 45. Map p 96.*

★★ Royal Lyceum Theatre WEST END   The Lyceum, built in 1883, has a most enviable reputation thanks to presentations that range from the most famous works of Shakespeare to hot new Scottish playwrights. It is home to the leading theatrical production company in the city, often attracting the best Scottish actors. *Grindlay St. (off*

Lothian Rd.). Box office ☎ *0131/248-4848; general inquiries 0131/238-4800. www.lyceum.org.uk. Tickets £8–£30. Bus: 1, 10, 11, 15, 16, 17, 24, or 34. Map p 96.*

★★★ **Traverse Theatre** WEST END   This local legend began in the 1960s as an experimental theater company that doubled as bohemian social club; it still produces contemporary drama at its height. The theater's bar is where you'll find the hippest dramatists and actors in the city. *10 Cambridge St. (off Lothian Rd.).* ☎ *0131/228-1404. www.traverse.co.uk. Tickets £5–£16. Bus: 1, 10, 11, 15, 16, 17, 24, or 34. Map p 96.*

Special Event

Military Tattoo   Taking place at the same time as the Edinburgh Festival, this is one of the city's more popular traditional spectacles. It features precision marching of not only Scottish regiments, but also soldiers and performers (including bands, drill teams, and gymnasts) from dozens of countries on the floodlit esplanade of Edinburgh Castle. *Tattoo Office, 32 Market St.* ☎ *0131/225-1188. www.edintattoo.co.uk. Tickets £23–£58.*

Usher Hall.

Spectator Sports

Easter Road Stadium   This 17,500-seat stadium, opened in 1893, is where the Hibernian Football Club (or simply Hibs, for short), one of Edinburgh's two soccer teams, plays. The club dates back to 1875, having first been organized by Irish immigrants (Hibernia's the Latin name for Ireland), and today is a feisty underdog in League matches. *Easter Road, toward Leith.* ☎ *0131/661-2159. www.hibs.co.uk. Tickets £12–£22. Bus: 1 or 35. Map p 96.*

Murrayfield Stadium   Opened in 1925, this is the country's national home for rugby and the largest stadium in Scotland, seating almost 68,000. The sport, which has an especially passionate following in Edinburgh, is played from autumn to

The World Comes to Edinburgh

The Edinburgh Festival (which is actually a few festivals running at once), held in August, is the cultural highlight of the year. The town is overrun during this time of year, so if you plan to arrive in August reserve your hotel well in advance. The **International Festival** box office is at The Hub, Castle Hill (☎ 0131/473-2000; www.eif.co.uk). **The Fringe** is based at 180 High St. (☎ 0131/226-0000; www.edfringe.com). Information on all the festivals is available at **www.edinburghfestivals.co.uk**. Ticket prices vary. For more on the Festivals, see p 102.

How to do the Edinburgh Festivals (Nearly!) for Free

Is it possible to soak up the energy released upon the city by the more than 20,000 performers without spending too much? Yes and here's how:

- Look out for the free **Fringe**—at the last count more than a fifth of the Fringe program (that lists over 2,400 shows) costs nothing.
- High culture at low prices—the **International Festival** brings together the best opera, theater, dance, and classical music companies from all over the world. Prices start at £14.
- Catch your breath at an art exhibition in one of Edinburgh's 50-plus galleries, many offering free entry.
- Fireworks—the world-famous **Royal Edinburgh Military Tattoo** culminates in a grand finale of fireworks at the castle esplanade. Grab a good viewing point and enjoy this dazzling spectacle.
- Free readings at the book festival—they happen early in the morning and late in the afternoon. You need a ticket though so arrive early.
- Cultural benefits—the ethnic-oriented **Edinburgh Mela Festival** (first weekend in September) costs less than £5 to enter and is a family hit at Leith Links.

spring, usually on Saturdays. Some of the most celebrated matches take place in the annual Six Nations competition comprising Scotland,

Military Tattoo.

Wales, England, Ireland, Italy, and France. *About 3km (1¾ miles) west of Edinburgh's city center (within walking distance from Haymarket station).* ☎ *0131/346-5000. www. scottishrugby.org. Tickets £5–£45. Bus: 12, 26, or 31. Map p 96.*

Tynecastle Stadium   Near Haymarket railway station, this facility is home to the evocatively named Heart of Midlothian Football Club. If that seems like a mouthful, just call them Hearts. Like Hibs, they haven't been a major force in Scottish sport for some time. *McLeod St.* ☎ *0131/ 663-1874. www.heartsfc.co.uk. Tickets £11–£29. Bus: 1, 2, 3, 21, 25, or 33. Map p 96.* ●

Edinburgh Hotels

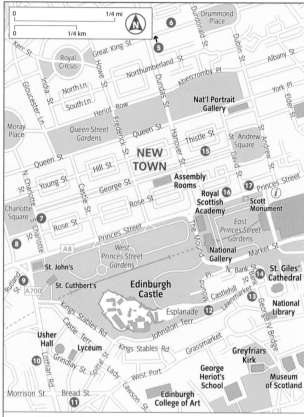

Abbey Hotel 19
Balmoral Hotel 20
The Bank Hotel 23
Barceló Edinburgh
    Carlton Hotel 22
The Bonham 3
Caledonian Hilton 9
Channings 4
The Chester Residence 1
The Edinburgh Residence 2
Fraser Suites 14
The George Hotel 15
The Glasshouse 18

Hotel Missoni 13
The Howard 6
Hudson Hotel 8
Macdonald Holyrood Hotel 25
Old Waverley Hotel 17
Point Hotel 11
Radisson Blu Hotel 24
Ramada Mount Royal 16
The Roxburghe Hotel 7
The Scotsman 21
Sheraton Grand Hotel & Spa 10
The Walton Guest House 5
The Witchery by the Castle 12

Previous Page: The Howard.

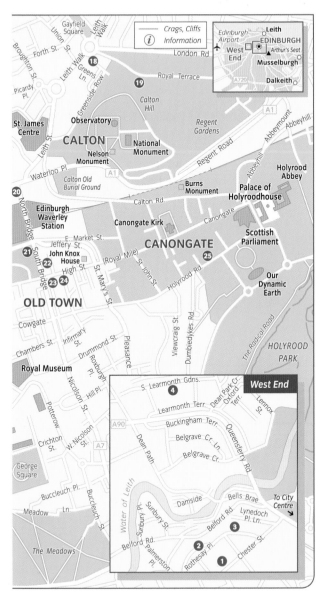

Crags, Cliffs

(i) Information

Edinburgh
Airport
West
End
Leith
EDINBURGH
Arthur's Seat
Musselburgh
A720
Dalkeith

Gayfield
Square
Leith
Walk
Union St.
Forth St.
Broughton St.
Picardy
Pl.
Leith Walk
Greenside Row
Greens
Ln.
London Rd.
Royal Terrace
18
19
St. James
Centre
Leith St.
Observatory
CALTON
Nelson
Monument
Calton
Hill
Regent
Gardens
National
Monument
Abbeymount
Abbeyhill
A1
A1
Holyrood
Abbey
Waterloo Pl.
Calton Old
Burial Ground
Regent Road
Abbeyhill
20
North Bridge
Edinburgh
Waverley
Station
Calton Rd.
Burns
Monument
Palace of
Holyroodhouse
Canongate Kirk
Canongate
21
E. Market St.
Jeffery St.
John Knox
House
CANONGATE
25
Scottish
Parliament
South Bridge
22
23 24
High St.
St. Mary's St.
(Royal Mile)
St. John St.
Holyrood Rd.
Our
Dynamic
Earth
OLD TOWN
Cowgate
Chambers St.
Infirmary
St.
Drummond St.
Roxburgh Pl.
Pleasance
Viewcraig St.
Dumbiedykes Rd.
The Radical Road
HOLYROOD
PARK
Royal Museum
Nicolson St.
Hill Pl.
Potterow
Crichton
St.
W. Nicolson St.
A7
George
Square
Buccleuch Pl.
Buccleuch St.
Meadow
Ln.
The Meadows

S. Learmonth Gdns.
4
Learmonth Terr.
Dean Park Cr.
Oxford Terr.
Lennox St.
West End
A90
Buckingham Terr.
Belgrave Cr. Ln.
Queensferry Rd.
Dean Path
Belgrave Cr.
Water of Leith
Damside
Bells Brae
Belford Rd.
Lynedoch
Pl. Ln.
To City
Centre
3
Sunbury Pl.
Sunbury St.
Belford Rd.
Palmerston
Pl.
2
Rothesay Pl.
1
Chester St.

Southside Hotels

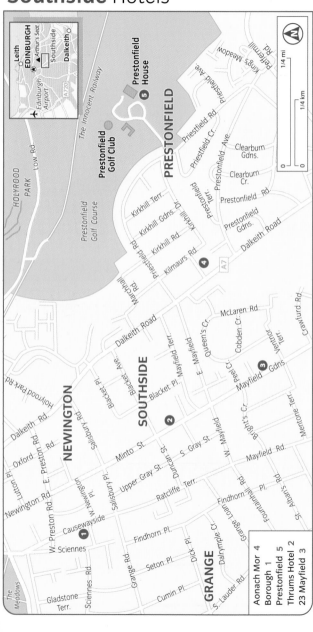

EDINBURGH
Leith
Arthur's Seat
Southside
Dalkeith
Edinburgh Airport
A720

Prestonfield House
5

The Innocent Railway

HOLYROOD PARK

Low Rd.

Prestonfield Golf Course

Prestonfield Golf Club

PRESTONFIELD

Kirkhill Terr.
Kirkhill Gdns.
Kirkhill Rd.
Kirkhill Dr.
Prestfield Rd.

Priestfield Rd.
Priestfield Cr.
Prestonfield Ave.
King's Meadow
Pefermill Rd.

Clearburn Gdns.
Clearburn Cr.

Prestonfield Terr.
Prestonfield Rd.
Prestonfield Gdns.

Kilmaurs Rd.
4

Dalkeith Road
A7

Marchhall Rd.

Dalkeith Road

McLaren Rd.

Crawfurd Rd.

Blacket Pl.
Blacket Ave.
Blacket Pl.
Mayfield Terr.

SOUTHSIDE
2

E. Mayfield
Queen's Cr.
Peel Ct.
Cobden Cr.
Ventnor Terr.
Mentone Terr.

Mayfield Gdns.
3

Holyrood Park Rd.

Dalkeith Rd.
Oxford Rd.
Lutton Pl.
E. Preston Rd.

NEWINGTON

Salisbury Rd.
Blacket Pl.

Minto St.
Upper Gray St.
Duncan St.
S. Gray St.
W. Mayfield

Bright's Cr.
Mayfield Rd.

Newington Rd.
W. Preston Rd.
E. Preston Rd.
W. Newington Pl.
Salisbury Pl.

Ratcliffe Terr.

Fountainhall Rd.
Findhorn Pl.
St. Alban's Rd.

Causewayside
1

Sciennes

Findhorn Pl.

GRANGE

Grange Rd.
Seton Pl.
Dick Pl.
Dalrymple Cr.
Grange Loan

Scienes Rd.
Gladstone Terr.
Cumin Pl.
S. Lauder Rd.

The Meadows

Aonach Mor 4
Borough 1
Prestonfield 5
Thrums Hotel 2
23 Mayfield 3

1/4 mi
1/4 km
0
0

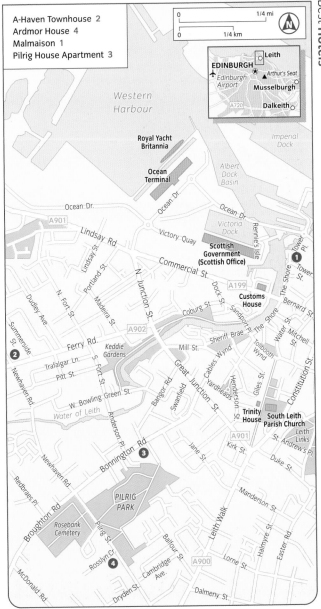

Leith Hotels

A-Haven Townhouse 2
Ardmor House 4
Malmaison 1
Pilrig House Apartment 3

0 _____ 1/4 mi
0 _____ 1/4 km

EDINBURGH
✈ Edinburgh Airport
Leith
★ Arthur's Seat
Musselburgh
A720
Dalkeith

Western Harbour

Royal Yacht Britannia

Ocean Terminal

Imperial Dock

Albert Dock Basin

Ocean Dr.

A901

Lindsay Rd.

Victory Quay

Ocean Dr.

Victoria Dock

Rennie's Isle

Scottish Government (Scottish Office)

Commercial St.

A199

Customs House

Tower Pl.

Tower St.

The Shore

Bernard St.

Dudley Ave.

N. Fort St.

Lindsay St.

Portland St.

Madeira St.

N. Junction St.

Dock St.

Sandport Pl.

The Shore

Water St.

Mitchell St.

Coburg St.

A902

Sheriff Brae

Tolbooth Wynd

Summerside St.

Newhaven Rd.

Ferry Rd.

Keddie Gardens

Mill St.

Cables Wynd

Yardheads

Henderson St.

Giles St.

Constitution St.

Trafalgar Ln.

S. Fort St.

Pitt St.

W. Bowling Green St.

Bangor Rd.

Swanfield

Great Junction St.

Trinity House

South Leith Parish Church

Leith Links

Water of Leith

Anderson Pl.

Bonnington Rd.

Jane St.

A901

Kirk St.

St. Andrew's Pl.

Duke St.

Newhaven Rd.

Redbraes Pl.

Broughton Rd.

PILRIG PARK

Rosebank Cemetery

Pilrig St.

Balfour St.

Manderson St.

Leith Walk

Halmyre St.

Easter Rd.

McDonald Rd.

Rosslyn Cr.

Cambridge Ave.

Dryden St.

A900

Lorne St.

Dalmeny St.

Hotel Best Bets

Best **Boutique Hotel**
★★ The Bonham, *35 Drumsheugh Gardens (p 109)*

Best **Traditional Hotel**
★ Caledonian Hilton, *Princes St. (p 110)*

Best **Spa**
★★ Sheraton Grand Hotel & Spa, *1 Festival Sq. (p 113)*

Best **Old Town Hotel**
★ The Scotsman, *20 N. Bridge (p 113)*

Best **New Town Hotel**
★★ The Howard, *34 Great King St. (p 111)*

Best **West End Hotel**
★★ The Edinburgh Residence, *7 Rothesay Terrace (p 111)*

Best **Hotel in Leith**
★★ Malmaison, *1 Tower Place (p 112)*

Best **View of the Castle**
Point Hotel, *34 Bread St. (p 112)*

Best **B&B**
★★ Ardmor House, *74 Pilrig St. (p 109)*

Best **Family Hotel**
A-Haven Townhouse, *180 Ferry Rd. (p 109)*

Best **Apartments**
★ The Chester Residence, *9 Chester St. (p 110)*

Best **Self-Catering**
★ Pilrig House Apartment, *Bonnington Rd. (p 112)*

Best **Guesthouse**
Aonach Mor, *14 Kilmaurs Terrace (p 109)*

Best **Hotel in a Quiet Neighborhood**
★★ Channings, *12–16 S. Learmonth Gardens (p 110)*

Best **Country House Hotel**
★★ Prestonfield, *Priestfield Rd. (p 112)*

A petite room at The Bonham.

Edinburgh **Hotels A to Z**

Sumptuously furnished room at the Balmoral Hotel.

Abbey Hotel NEW TOWN On the slopes of Calton Hill, this small hotel (previously called the Greenside) received mixed reviews in the past. After the rechristening though, it seems that opinion is rising. It is well located and the building retains some of its traditional Georgian features. *9 Royal Terrace* ☎ *0131/557-0022. www.abbeyhoteledinburgh. co.uk. 15 units. Double £60–£130. AE, DC, MC, V. Bus: 1, 4, 5, or 15. Map p 104.*

kids A-Haven Townhouse LEITH The A-Haven is a semi-detached gray-stone Victorian building, with traditionally furnished rooms, some of which are large enough to accommodate families. Parents may appreciate the nearby park too. *180 Ferry Rd.* ☎ *0131/554-6559. www. a-haven.co.uk. 14 units. Doubles £74–£130; family room £70–£130. AE, MC, V. Bus: 14. Map p 107.*

★ **Aonach Mor** SOUTHSIDE A well-priced, family-run guesthouse located in a proud row of three-storey Victorian terraced houses, away from the bustle of the city center. Some rooms offer a view of Arthur's Seat. *14 Kilmaurs Terrace (at*

Dalkeith Rd.). ☎ *0131/667-8694. www.aonachmor.com. 7 units. Doubles £60–£140. MC, V. Bus: 3, 8, or 29. Map p 106.*

★★ **Ardmor House** LEITH This gay-friendly boutique B&B is decorated with plush, modern furnishings amid bay windows and period settees. The owners also have two highly rated self-catering apartments in New Town. *74 Pilrig St. (near Leith Walk).* ☎ *0131/554-4944. www.ardmor house.com. 5 units. Doubles £75– £145. MC, V. Bus: 11. Map p 107.*

★★ **Balmoral Hotel** NEW TOWN Opened in 1902, this is one of the grandest hotels in Britain, with kilted doormen waiting to greet you on arrival. All rooms are sumptuously furnished; some are palatial. *1 Princes St.* ☎ *0131/556-2414. www. thebalmoralhotel.com. 188 units. Doubles from £360. AE, DC, MC, V. Bus: 3, 8, 22, 25, or 30. Map p 104.*

The Bank Hotel OLD TOWN This hotel—housed in a former Bank of Scotland branch—offers better value than many of its local competitors. The guest rooms are dedicated to the works of famous Scots, including Robert Burns and

The Bank Hotel.

Alexander Graham Bell. *1 S. Bridge St.* ☎ *0131/622-6800. www.festival-inns.co.uk. 9 units. Doubles £114–£185. AE, MC, V. Bus: 35. Map p 104.*

Barceló Edinburgh Carlton Hotel OLD TOWN   This baronial pile has seen substantial upgrades over the years, enlarging some rooms to make space for private bathrooms with a tub and shower. Furnishings are tasteful with a sub-dued modern simplicity. Light sleep-ers should request a room at the rear. *19 N. Bridge.* ☎ *0131/472-3000. www.barcelo-hotels.co.uk. 189 units. Double from £150. AE, DC, MC, V. Bus: 3, 8, 14, or 29. Map p 104.*

★★ The Bonham WEST END
One of the city's most stylish hotels, the Bonham has individually fur-nished rooms with luxurious uphol-steries and modern bathrooms fitted with deep tubs, showers, and elegant toiletries: a hip blend of old and new. *35 Drumsheugh Gardens.* ☎ *0131/226-6050. www.thebonham. com. 48 units. Doubles £125–£280; suite £220–£400. AE, DC, MC, V. Bus: 19 or 37. Map p 104.*

Borough SOUTHSIDE   While admittedly on the small side, the rooms in this boutique hotel are individually designed with high ceil-ings, casement windows, and stylish furnishings. The bar on the ground floor is equally fashionable. *72–80 Causewayside.* ☎ *0131/668-2255. www.theboroughhotel.com. 12 units. Doubles £50–£150. MC, V. Bus: 3, 5, 7, or 31. Map p 106.*

★ Caledonian Hilton WEST END
This city landmark is blessed with commanding views of Edinburgh Castle. An elegant Edwardian atmosphere pervades its public areas and the top-end guest rooms are spacious and well-appointed. *Princes St. (at Lothian Rd.).* ☎ *0131/ 222-8888. www.hilton.co.uk/ caledonian. 251 units. Doubles from £199. AE, DC, MC, V. Bus: 12, 25, or 33. Map p 104.*

★★ Channings NEW TOWN
Five Edwardian terrace houses were combined to create this coun-try-house-style hotel. One of the townhouses was once home to Arctic explorer Ernest Shackelton, and top-floor suites are named in his and other explorers' honor. *12–16 S. Lear-month Gardens (near Queensferry Rd.).* ☎ *0131/623-9302. www. channings.co.uk. 41 units. Doubles £115–£250. AE, MC, V. Bus: 37. Map p 104.*

★ The Chester Residence WEST END   The serviced apartments in

A suite bath tub at Channings Hotel.

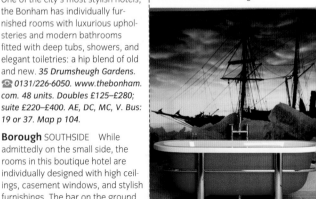

the Chester vary in size, but all sit in the luxury category. The 'Mews' flats have their own private gardens, and in-house spa treatments are available on request. *9 Rothsay Pl.* ☎ *0131/226-2075. www.chester-residence.com. 20 units. £165–£500. MC, V. Bus: 19, 36, or 41. Map p 104.*

★★ The Edinburgh Residence WEST END The grand staircase and classic wood paneling in the hallways lead you to the spacious suites, decked out with cherry wood furniture, botanical prints, and understated, traditional soft furnishings—and even larger Townhouse Apartments—at this top-end hotel. *7 Rothesay Terrace.* ☎ *0131/226-3380. www.theedinburghresidence. com. 29 units. Suites £125–£400. AE, MC, V. Bus: 19, 36, or 41. Map p 104.*

★ Fraser Suites OLD TOWN A relative newcomer with everything from cozy Classic Rooms to split level Executive Suites and luxury apartments. Classy and well located near the Royal Mile. *12–26 Giles St.* ☎ *0131/221-7200 www.edinburgh. frasershospitality.com. 75 units. Doubles £300; suites from £330. AE, MC, V. Bus: 23, 27, 35, 42, or 67. Map p 104.*

The George Hotel NEW TOWN The buildings that house this elegant inn in the heart of the city were first erected in the 1780s. Today, rooms are decorated with deluxe furnishings in fashionably earthy shades of eggplant and brown, with plasma TVs and other mod-cons. *9–21 George St.* ☎ *0131/225-1251. www.principal-hayley.com. 195 units. Doubles £185–£320. AE, DC, MC, V. Bus: 24, 28, or 45. Map p 104.*

★ The Glasshouse NEW TOWN Among the top boutique hotels of Edinburgh, the Glasshouse combines old and new, with an impressive stone church facade harmonizing with the modern glass structure.

Many of the sleek, modern bedrooms offer fine views over the city. *2 Greenside Place (Leith Walk).* ☎ *0131/525-8200. www.theeton collection.co.uk. 65 units. Doubles £355. Bus: 5, 14, or 22. Map p 104.*

Hotel Missoni OLD TOWN This is a highly regarded new hotel that would not be out of place in Rome's most fashionable inner-city districts. Designed by Rosita Missoni (of the Varese-based knitware/home furnishings company), the scheme of black, white, and silver is punctuated by bright swatches of color. *George IV Bridge.* ☎ *0131/220-6666. www.hotelmissoni.com. 136 units. Double £200–£300. AE, MC, V. Bus: 23, 27, 41, 45, or 67. Map p 104.*

★★ The Howard NEW TOWN Georgian era townhouses with a definite aura of privacy make this one of the most discreet top-rated hotels. Service is a hallmark of The Howard, with a team of butlers who tend to guests' individual needs. *34 Great King St.* ☎ *0131/557-3500. www.thehoward.com. 18 units. Doubles £185–£300. AE, DC, MC, V. Bus: 23 or 27. Map p 104.*

Hudson Hotel NEW TOWN With a happening bar and nightclub, this boutique hotel is also well located at the western end of Princes Street. The smart rooms have Egyptian cotton bedding, wireless Internet, and flatscreen TVs. *7–11 Hope St.* ☎ *0131/622-6800. www.festival-inns.co.uk/hudson.html 31 units. Double £150. AE, MC, V. Bus: 19, 36, 41, or 47. Map p 104.*

★ Macdonald Holyrood Hotel OLD TOWN This impressive and stylish hotel is only minutes from the heart of Old Town. Bedrooms are luxurious, with sumptuous furnishings and posh toiletries; the Club Floor is one of the best high-end retreats in town—a self-contained, kids-free wing with extra secure rooms and a shared library. *81 Holyrood Rd.* ☎ *0844/879-9028. www.macdonaldhotels.co.uk. 156 units. Doubles from £90. AE, DC, MC, V. Bus: 35. Map p 104.*

★★ **Malmaison** LEITH This hip, unpretentious boutique hotel with minimalist decor was once the seaman's mission where salty dogs could get a room for the night and a meal in the morning in the old harbor district. Rooms are average in size but individually designed and well equipped. *1 Tower Place, Leith.* ☎ *0131/468-5000. www.malmaison.com. 100 units. Doubles £120–£180. AE, DC, MC, V. Bus: 16, 22, 35, or 36. Map p 107.*

Old Waverley Hotel NEW TOWN It first opened in 1848 as a temperance hotel opposite the Scott Monument. Today, this landmark offers comfortable, traditionally styled guest rooms with flatscreen TVs. What you're really paying for here is the excellent location. *43 Princes St.* ☎ *0131/556-4648. www.old waverley.co.uk. 66 units. Doubles £239. AE, DC, MC, V. Bus: 15, 19, 26, 37, or 44. Map p 104.*

★ **Pilrig House Apartment** LEITH Robert Louis Stevenson played in this 17th-century mansion's gardens as a child. Nowadays, these self-catering apartments are ideal for those who seek a quieter city retreat in elegant surroundings. It is only a short stroll from here to the center. *Pilrig House Close, Bonnington Rd.* ☎ *0131/554-4794. www.pilrighouse apartment.co.uk. 3 units; £90–£250. MC, V. Bus: 11 or 36. Map p 107.*

Point Hotel WEST END Standard rooms here may feel a bit cozy, but the premium units are much more spacious and several have views of the castle. If your taste in decor is more stainless steel and brushed chrome than Scottish tartan and antiques, this is the place to stay. *32 Bread St.* ☎ *0131/221-5555. www. pointhoteledinburgh.co.uk. 130 units. Doubles £100–£160. AE, DC, MC, V. Bus: 2 or 35. Map p 104.*

★★ **Prestonfield** SOUTHSIDE Boasting Jacobean splendor amid 5.3 hectares (13 acres) of gardens, pastures, and woodlands, this 17th-century hotel has hosted luminaries ranging from Benjamin Franklin to Sean Connery. The guest rooms boast Bose sound systems and plasma flatscreen TVs. *Priestfield Rd.* ☎ *0131/225–7800. www. prestonfield.com. 28 units. Doubles £195–£440. AE, MC, V. Bus: 2, 14, or 30. Map p 106.*

Hostels: Not only for Youths

A few hostels have private rooms, too. Your best bets include the **Edinburgh Central,** a five-star hostel, which is part of the Scottish Youth Hostel Association. Single rooms with en-suite facilities start at £34 and twins are £51 and upward, depending on the season. It is located at 9 Haddington Pl., Edinburgh EH7 4AL; ☎ 0845/293-7373; www.edinburghcentral.org. Another option is **Budget Backpackers,** at 37–39 Cowgate, Edinburgh EH1 1JR. Twin rooms are around £25 per person. For reservations, don't leave to the last minute, and phone ☎ 0131/226-6351; www.budget backpackers.com.

Hip decor at Malmaison.

★ Radisson Blu Hotel OLD TOWN
The preferred major hotel in central
Old Town, this thoroughly modern
facility (don't let the baronial exterior
fool you) is also one of the best
equipped, with a leisure club and an
indoor pool. Most bedrooms are spacious and well decorated. *80 High St.*
☎ *0131/557-9797. www.radisson.
com. 238 units. Doubles £180. AE, DC,
MC, V. Bus: 35. Map p 104.*

Ramada Mount Royal NEW
TOWN   There aren't necessarily
many frills at the Ramada, but the
streamlined guest rooms offer a perfectly acceptable level of comfort for
a short stay. It would be hard to find
a more central location across from
Princes Street Gardens. *53 Princes
St.* ☎ *0131/225-7161. www.ramada
jarvis.co.uk. 158 units. Doubles
£125–£180. AE, DC, MC, V. Bus: 15,
19, 26, 37, or 44. Map p 104.*

★ The Roxburghe Hotel NEW
TOWN   Its classy atmosphere
starts in the elegant lobby, which
has an ornate ceiling and antique
furnishings. The largest rooms—in
the hotel's original wing—have
imposing fireplaces, but units in the
newer wing benefit from more modern bathrooms. *38 Charlotte St. (at
George St.).* ☎ *0844/879-9063.
www.macdonaldhotels.co.uk/
roxburghe. 198 units. Doubles £105–
£270. AE, DC, MC, V. Bus: 19, 36, 41,
or 47. Map p 104.*

★ The Scotsman OLD TOWN
One of the brightest and most stylish hotels in Edinburgh. Traditional
decor and cutting-edge design are
harmoniously wed in the 1904 baronial building (which was once home
to the newspaper that lent the hotel
its name), a city landmark since it
was first constructed. *20 North
Bridge.* ☎ *0131/556-5565. www.
scotsmanhotels.com. 68 units. Doubles £150–£300. AE, DC, MC, V. Bus:
3, 8, 14, or 29. Map p 104.*

**★★ Sheraton Grand Hotel &
Spa** WEST END   Elegant, with soaring public rooms and rich carpeting,
the Sheraton boasts an enviable
location in the proverbial shadow of
Edinburgh Castle. Guest rooms are

Old-style character at Prestonfield.

Theatrical room at The Witchery by the Castle.

well equipped whilst the hotel has the best spa and leisure facilities (including a rooftop indoor/outdoor pool) in the city. *1 Festival Sq. (at Lothian Rd.).* ☎ *0131/229-9131. www.sheraton.com. 260 units. Doubles £150–£360. AE, DC, MC, V. Bus: 10, 22, or 30. Map p 104.*

kids Thrums Hotel SOUTHSIDE Located in the Newington district, less than a kilometer from the Meadows, Thrums has high-ceilinged guest rooms with antique furnishings. Some units are set aside as family rooms while the garden offers an outdoor play area. *14–15 Minto St.* ☎ *0131/667-5545. www. thrumshotel.com. 15 units. Doubles £55–£110. MC, V. Bus: 3, 8, or 29. Map p 106.*

23 Mayfield SOUTHSIDE Run since 2008 by the former owners of Aonach Mor (p 109), this handsome Victorian guesthouse is about a mile from the center of the city. All rooms include beautiful mahogany furniture, and the Jacobean quarters have four-poster beds. *23 Mayfield Gardens.* ☎ *0131/667-5806. www.23mayfield. co.uk. 9 units. Double £80–£130. MC, V. Bus: 5, 7, 8, or 29. Map p 106.*

The Walton Guest House NEW TOWN This elegant Georgian guesthouse sits at the heart of Edinburgh's less frenetic northern New Town. The location means guests have a short walk up the hill to the busier streets of New Town proper. *79 Dundas St.* ☎ *0131/556-1137. www.waltonhotel.com. 10 units. Double £90–£150. Bus 23 or 27. Map p 104.*

★★★ The Witchery by the Castle OLD TOWN Part of the famous restaurant (p 82), the overnight accommodations in the Witchery include romantic, sumptuous, and theatrically decorated suites with Gothic antiques and elaborate tapestries. The much-lauded property has played host to a long list of celebrity guests. *Castlehill.* ☎ *0131/225-5613. www.the witchery.com. 7 units. Suites £325. AE, DC, MC, V. Bus: 28. Map p 104.* ●

The Chain Gang

If you're the type of traveler who thinks of hotels as just places to lay one's head at night, some of the better deals in town are found at the no-frills chains. In the heart of Old Town, try the **Ibis,** 6 Hunter Sq., Edinburgh EH1 1QW (☎ 0131/240-7000; www.ibishotel.com), where rooms generally are below £100. In the West End, the **Premier Inn,** 1 Morrison Link, Edinburgh EH3 8DN (☎ 0870/238-3319; www. premiertravelinn.co.uk), is modern and functional with rooms at around £85, although its Leith branch is cheaper still at £65.

The Best in One Day

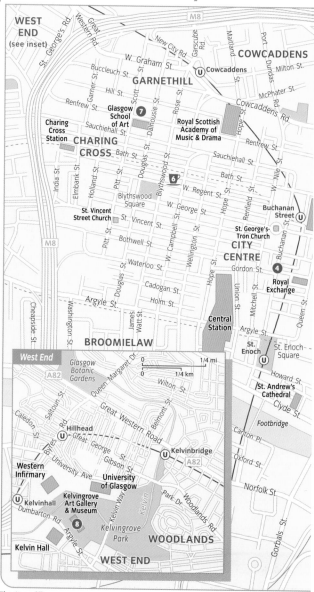

WEST
END
(see inset)

M8

Garscube Rd

New City Rd

Maitland

Port Dundas Rd

Milton St.

COWCADDENS

St. George's Rd.

Great Western Rd.

W. Graham St.

U Cowcaddens

McPhater St.

Buccleuch St.

GARNETHILL

Cowcaddens Rd.

Hope St.

Garnet St.

Hill St.

Scott St.

Rose St.

Renfrew St.

Glasgow
School
of Art **7**

Dalhousie St.

Royal Scottish
Academy of
Music & Drama

Renfrew St.

Charing
Cross
Station

Sauchiehall St.

CHARING
CROSS

Sauchiehall St.

Sauchiehall St.

Bath St.

Douglas St.

Blythswood St.

Bath St.

W. Nile St.

India St.

Elmbank St.

Holland St.

Pitt St.

Blythswood
Square

W. Regent St. **6**

Hope St.

Renfield St.

Buchanan
Street U

St. Vincent
Street Church

St. Vincent St.

W. George St.

St. George's-
Tron Church

Bothwell St.

W. Campbell St.

Wellington St.

CITY
CENTRE

Buchanan St.

M8

Waterloo St.

Gordon St.

4

Royal
Exchange

Queen St.

Douglas St.

Cadogan St.

Hope St.

Mitchell St.

Argyle St.

Holm St.

Union St.

Central
Station

Argyle St.

St.
Enoch
U

St. Enoch
Square

Cheapside St.

Washington St.

James Watt St.

BROOMIELAW

Howard St.

St. Andrew's
Cathedral

West End

Glasgow
Botanic
Gardens

A82

Queen Margaret Dr.

0   1/4 mi

0   1/4 km

Wilton St.

Clyde St.

Footbridge

Caledon St.

Saltoun St.

Great Western Road

Belmont St.

Carlton Pl.

U Hillhead

Great George St.

Gibson St.

U Kelvinbridge

Oxford St.

Byres Rd.

University Ave.

A82

Norfolk St.

Western
Infirmary

University
of Glasgow

Kelvin Way

Park Dr.

Woodlands Rd.

U Kelvinhall

Kelvingrove Art Gallery
& Museum

Kelvin

Kelvin

Dumbarton Rd.

8

Argyle St.

Kelvingrove
Park

WOODLANDS

Gorbals St.

Kelvin Hall

WEST END

The Armadillo.

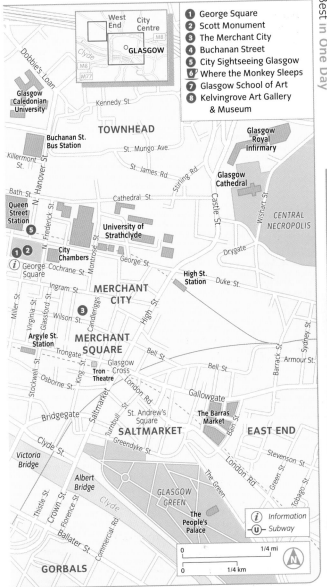

1 George Square
2 Scott Monument
3 The Merchant City
4 Buchanan Street
5 City Sightseeing Glasgow
6 Where the Monkey Sleeps
7 Glasgow School of Art
8 Kelvingrove Art Gallery & Museum

West End
City Centre
GLASGOW
M8
Clyde
M8
M77

Dobbie's Loan

Glasgow Caledonian University

Kennedy St.

Kennedy St.

TOWNHEAD

Glasgow Royal Infirmary

Buchanan St. Bus Station

St. Mungo Ave.

Killermont St.

Bath St.

St. James Rd.

Stirling Rd.

Glasgow Cathedral

Queen Street Station

N. Hanover St.

Cathedral St.

Castle St.

Wishart St.

CENTRAL NECROPOLIS

5

Frederick St.

University of Strathclyde

N. Frederick St.

City Chambers

Montrose St.

Drygate

1 2

George Square

Cochrane St.

George St.

High St. Station

Duke St.

i

Ingram St.

MERCHANT CITY

High St.

Miller St.

Virginia St.

Glassford St.

Wilson St.

3

Candleriggs

Argyle St. Station

MERCHANT SQUARE

Trongate

King St.

Glasgow Cross

Tron Theatre

Bell St.

Bell St.

Barrack St.

Sydney St.

Armour St.

Stockwell St.

Osborne St.

Saltmarket

Turnbull St.

London Rd.

Gallowgate

The Barras Market

Bain St.

EAST END

Bridgegate

Clyde St.

St. Andrew's Square

SALTMARKET

Greendyke St.

London Rd.

Stevenson St.

Green St.

Tobago St.

Victoria Bridge

Albert Bridge

Thistle St.

Crown St.

Florence St.

Ballater St.

Commercial Rd.

Clyde

GLASGOW GREEN

The Green

The People's Palace

i Information
U Subway

0   1/4 mi
0   1/4 km

N

GORBALS

Scotland's largest city possesses a very different ambience to Edinburgh, less pristine and quaint, more modern and sparky. To see most of this vibrant city (pronounced *glaaz-go*) in a single day is impossible, but you can take in the major highlights. Begin with the Victorian splendor of the city center, and finish with a foray into the salubrious West End. START: **Buchanan St. underground station.**

George Square is Glasgow's central plaza and popular meeting place.

❶ ★ George Square. This is the city's central plaza (originally laid out in 1782) named for King George III. It's a popular meeting place and home to a number of 19th-century statues commemorating famous Scots and Brits. At the eastern end is the opulent **City Chambers** (opened in 1888), and near the southwest corner of the square is the city's well-run main tourist office. ⏱ *30–45 min.*

❷ Scott Monument. The most imposing of George Square's monuments is right in the center—a Doric column, 25m (82-ft.) high, topped by Sir Walter Scott. It was the first monument built to honor the Edinburgh-born author, about 5 years after his death in 1832. ⏱ *10 min. In George Sq.*

❸ ★★ The Merchant City. This is Glasgow's equivalent of New York's SoHo district, with converted warehouses set amid hip shops, galleries, trendy cafes, bars, and restaurants. Begun as a New Town development in the 1700s, this area also abuts the historic core of Glasgow along the High Street—though all remnants of the city's medieval past were long ago demolished. ⏱ *1 hr. Train: Argyle St.*

❹ ★★ Buchanan Street. This pedestrian-only boulevard usually teems with people, and stretches from the River Clyde, up a gentle slope, to the Glasgow Royal Concert Hall. If you're a fan of retail therapy, your shopping trip should probably begin—and possibly end—here. ⏱ *30 min–2 hr. Underground: Buchanan St.*

❺ ★★ City Sightseeing Glasgow. Tours on the brightly colored, open-topped buses hit all of the city's principal highlights and also offer a good general orientation to the city. The tour guides' observations are also often hilarious—as entertaining as informative—they beat the taped version hands down. You can hop on and off as you please. ⏱ 1¾ hr. George Sq. ☎ 0141/204-0444. www.scotguide.com. Tickets £11 adults, £9 seniors/students, £5 child, £25 family. Daily Apr–Oct every 15-30 min, 9:30am–5pm (7:30pm July to August); Nov–Mar every 30 min, 10am–3:30pm. Underground: Buchanan St.

Founded by artistic types (including two graduates from the nearby Art School), **6** ★ **Where the Monkey Sleeps**, a singular cafe-cum-gallery, is one of the best daytime stops for toasties, soups, sandwiches, and bagels. 182 W. Regent St. ☎ 0141/226-3406. www.monkeysleeps.com. £.

7 ★★★ **Glasgow School of Art.** This magnificent building on Garnethill in the city's Commercial Centre is the highlight of the **Charles Rennie Mackintosh** (1868–1928) architecture trail. The sublime work by Mackintosh is even more remarkable when you

consider that he wasn't even 30 years of age when he designed the school's principal building. It remains a working—and much respected—school of art and design. Take the tour to see all the interiors, stopping by the basement shop for gifts and unique souvenirs. ⏱ 1½ hr. See p 130, **2**.

8 ★★ kids **Kelvingrove Art Gallery & Museum.** The Spanish Baroque-style Kelvingrove (built in 1901 of red sandstone) is the stirring soul of the city's art collection, one of the best amassed by a municipality in Europe. It is the most visited gallery and museum in the UK, outside of London. The art (from French Impressionists to Spanish Surrealists) is great, but there is much more to see here, with exhibits on Scottish and Glasgow history, armory, and war, and on natural history too. There's also some humor: Watch out for the furry haggis animal. ⏱ 2½ hr. Argyle St. ☎ 0141/276-9599. www.glasgowmuseums.com. Free admission, except for some temporary exhibits. Mon–Thurs, Sat 10am–5pm; Fri, Sun 11am–5pm. Bus: 9, 16, 42, or 62. Underground: Kelvinhall.

The Kelvingrove Art Gallery and Museum.

The Best in Two Days

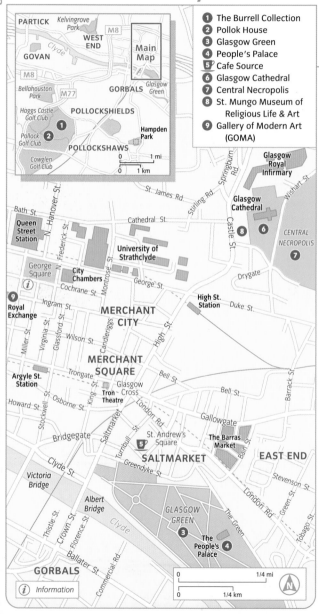

1. The Burrell Collection
2. Pollok House
3. Glasgow Green
4. People's Palace
5. Cafe Source
6. Glasgow Cathedral
7. Central Necropolis
8. St. Mungo Museum of Religious Life & Art
9. Gallery of Modern Art (GOMA)

The River Clyde runs through Glasgow, dividing the city into two sections. After spending a day exploring the north side, head across the river to the vaunted Burrell Collection for world-class art, before returning to the north banks for a sampling of the city's hot spots for history and culture. START: **Take suburban train to Pollokshaws West or bus 45, 47, or 57.**

Explore the treasures of wealthy industrialist Sir William Burrell.

❶ ★★★ The Burrell Collection. This custom-built museum houses close to 9,000 treasures left to the City of Glasgow by wealthy industrialist Sir William Burrell in 1958 (though the building itself didn't open until 1983). Burrell's tastes were eclectic: Chinese ceramics, French paintings from the 1800s, stained-glass church windows, medieval stone doorways, and tapestries. One major highlight is an original casting of Rodin's *The Thinker*. Other important features not to miss are the works by Degas, Cézanne, and Whistler. ⏱ *2 hr. Pollok Country Park, 2060 Pollokshaws Rd.* ☎ *0141/287-2550. www.glasgowmuseums.com. Free admission. Mon–Thurs, Sat 10am–5pm; Fri, Sun 11am–5pm.*

❷ ★ Pollok House. Make a quick stop here: It is only a 5 to 10 minute walk from the Burrell. This handsome 18th-century mansion, on an estate held by the Maxwell family for over 6 centuries, offers a snapshot of historic country life on what once were the fringes of the city. It's also home to a first-class collection of Spanish art, including works by Goya and El Greco. ⏱ *45 min. Pollok Country Park.* ☎ *0141/616-6410. www.glasgowmuseums.com. Free admission. Daily 10am–5pm. Adjacent to the Burrell in Pollok Country Park.*

❸ ★ kids Glasgow Green. Glasgow Green is the city's oldest park, dating to late medieval times. Its landmarks include the **People's Palace and Winter Garden** and the 44m (143-ft.) **Nelson's Monument,** which was erected in 1806 in honor of Admiral Horatio Nelson—30 years before the more famous

The People's Palace.

Nelson's Column in London was built. At the park's eastern end, Venice's Doges' Palace is virtually recreated in the old **Templeton Carpet Factory** (built 1889), which now houses a micro-brewery and bar (p 162). ⏱ *1 hr. Greendyke St. (east of Saltmarket).* ☎ *0141/287-5098. www.glasgow.gov.uk. Free admission. Daily dawn–dusk. Underground: St. Enoch. Bus: 16, 18, 40, 61, 62, or 64.*

④ ★ **kids People's Palace.** This museum, first opened in 1898, showcases Glasgow's social history, with displays on working-class life in the city, especially since the industrial age. In front of the museum is the heavily sculpted **Doulton Fountain,** the largest terra-cotta fountain in the world. Attached to the museum is the **Victorian Winter Gardens** with a fine collection of delicate and semi-hardy plants. ⏱ *1½ hr. Glasgow Green.* ☎ *0141/554-0223. www.glasgowmuseums.com. Free admission. Mon–Sat 10am–5pm; Fri, Sun 11am–5pm. Bus: 16, 18, 43, 64, or 263.*

⑤ **Cafe Source,** in the basement of the architecturally outstanding St. Andrew's in the Square Church (see p 163), serves up plates of Scotch pie, West Coast mussels, or croque monsieur. *St. Andrew's Sq.* ☎ *0141/548-6020. www.standrews inthesquare.com. £.*

⑥ ★★ **Glasgow Cathedral (St. Mungo's).** Mainland Scotland's only complete medieval cathedral (dating to the 13th century), this is the country's most important pre-Reformation ecclesiastical edifice. Unlike other Roman Catholic cathedrals, St. Mungo's survived the Protestant revolt practically intact. The one major blow to the structure was done at the hands of Victorian era builders, who in the course of renovations had a tower removed. The lower church is the oldest portion of the building, with a vaulted Gothic-style crypt that's among the finest in Europe and houses the tomb of Glasgow's patron saint Mungo (d. 614). ⏱ *1½ hr. Castle St. (at High St.).* ☎ *0141/552-6891. www.historic-scotland.gov.uk. Free* admission. *Apr–Sept Mon–Sat 9:30am–6pm, Sun 1–5pm; Oct–Mar Mon–Sat 9:30am–4pm, Sun 1–4pm. Bus: 11, 36, 37, 38, 42, or 89. Train: High St.*

⑦ ★★ Central Necropolis. Built on a proud hill above Glasgow Cathedral and patterned on Paris's Père Lachaise, this graveyard was opened in the 1830s. You won't be able to miss the 62m (203-ft.) monument to John Knox at the top of the hill; it was erected in 1825. The cemetery's numerous Victorian-style monuments are excellent—as are the views of Glasgow. 🕐 *1 hr. Adjacent to Glasgow Cathedral. Free admission. Daily dawn–dusk. Bus: 11, 36, 37, 38, 42, or 89. Train: High St.*

View from Central Necropolis.

⑧ St. Mungo Museum of Religious Life & Art. Opened in 1993, this eclectic museum of spirituality (treating all religions equally) is located next to Glasgow Cathedral on the site where the Bishop's Castle—the mansion in which the Catholic archbishops of Glasgow once resided—stood until the 17th century. Art and artifacts include a 16th-century European carving of the virgin and child, and there is a Zen garden too. 🕐 *45 min. 2 Castle St.* ☎ *0141/553-2557. Free admission. Tue–Thurs, Sat 10am–5pm; Fri,* *Sun 11am–5pm. Bus: 11, 36, 37, 38, 42, or 89. Train: High St.*

⑨ ★ Gallery of Modern Art (GOMA). GOMA is housed in a neoclassical building that once served as the city's Royal Exchange and was originally built as a mansion for an 18th-century tobacco magnate. Opened in 1996, the modern art gallery focuses on artwork from 1950 onward. The permanent collection has works by Uglow, Spencer, and Bellany, as well as art from the 1980s 'new Glasgow Boys' such as Steven Campbell and Adrian Wiszniewski. 🕐 *1 hr. Royal Exchange Sq., Queen St.* ☎ *0141/229-1996. www.glasgowmuseums.com. Free admission. Mon–Wed, Sat 10am–5pm; Thurs 10am–8pm; Fri, Sun 11am–5pm. Underground: Buchanan St.*

Glasgow's medieval cathedral.

The Best **in Three Days**

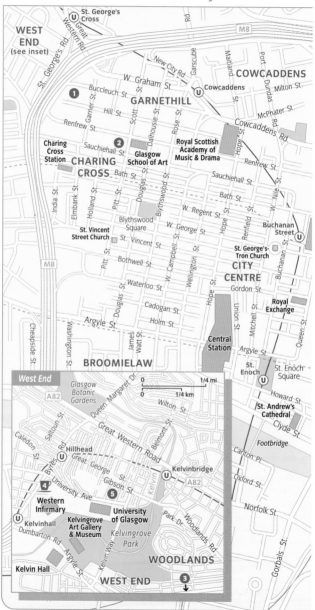

WEST END
(see inset)

St. George's
Cross

COWCADDENS

Cowcaddens

GARNETHILL

Royal Scottish
Academy of
Music & Drama

Charing
Cross
Station

**CHARING
CROSS**

Glasgow
School of Art

Buchanan
Street

St. Vincent
Street Church

Blythswood
Square

St. George's-
Tron Church

**CITY
CENTRE**

Royal
Exchange

BROOMIELAW

Central
Station

St.
Enoch

St. Enoch
Square

West End

Glasgow
Botanic
Gardens

St. Andrew's
Cathedral

Footbridge

Hillhead

Kelvinbridge

Western
Infirmary

University
of Glasgow

Kelvinhall

Kelvingrove
Art Gallery
& Museum

Kelvingrove
Park

Kelvin Hall

WOODLANDS

WEST END

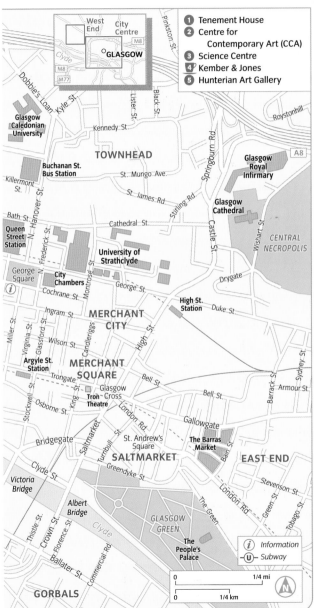

1 Tenement House
2 Centre for Contemporary Art (CCA)
3 Science Centre
4 Kember & Jones
5 Hunterian Art Gallery

The history of Glasgow is a bit checkered, at least from a visitor's point of view. In the 18th century, the writer Daniel Defoe gave praise to the city's charm, but by the end of the 19th century, it had become a smoke-ridden industrial powerhouse rather than a place of beauty. Today, the grime has gone and heavy manufacturing has moved on, leaving a modern metropolis. START: **Garnethill; take underground to Cowcaddens or bus 11, 20, or 66.**

The atrium café inside the Centre for Contemporary Art.

❶ ★ **Tenement House.** Tenements (or apartment buildings) are what many Glaswegians have lived in from the mid-19th-century onward. This 'museum' is a typical tenement flat of the 1890s, preserved with many original fixtures and fittings: coal fires, box bed in the kitchen, and gas lamps. Its former resident, Miss Agnes Toward, rarely threw anything out from 1911 to 1965, so there are displays of all sorts of memorabilia. 🕐 *1 hr. 145 Buccleuch St.* ☎ *0141/333-0183. www.nts.org.uk. Admission £6 adults; £5 seniors, students, and*

children; £15.50 family. Mar–Oct daily 1–5pm. Closed Nov–Feb. Bus: 20, 59, or 60. Underground: Cowcaddens.

❷ ★ **Centre for Contemporary Art (CCA).** A leading proponent of conceptual art in Glasgow, the CCA was established in 1992 and is home to a diverse (and often-changing) lineup of experimental art and film. The center's modern interiors are contained in a building designed by Alexander 'Greek' Thomson in the mid-1800s. If you fancy a coffee, the central, atrium-like space has an excellent cafe. 🕐 *1 hr. 350 Sauchiehall St.* ☎ *0141/352-4900. www. cca-glasgow.com. Free admission. Tues–Fri 11am–6pm; Sat 10am–6pm. Bus: 16, 18, 44, or 57. Underground: Cowcaddens.*

❸ 🔳 **Science Centre.** The futuristic-looking edifice of the center's main building is a focal point of Glasgow's drive to redevelop the rundown former docklands. The main themes inside are 21st-century challenges and Glasgow's contribution to science and technology in the past, present, and future. The center also has a planetarium and IMAX theater. 🕐 *2 hr. 50 Pacific Quay.* ☎ *0141/420-5010. www. glasgowsciencecentre.org. Admission £7.95 adults, £5.95 child, £2 car parking. Daily 10am–6pm (Nov to mid-Mar Mon–Sat 10am–5pm). Bus: 89 or 90. Train: Exhibition Centre and walk across the footbridge over the Clyde. Underground: Cessnock.*

Part deli and part cafe, **4** **Kember & Jones** is set in the heart of the West End's main street and is a fine stop for freshly made sandwiches, soups, salads, and cakes. *134 Byres Rd.* ☎ *0141/337-3851. www.kemberandjones.co.uk. £.*

5 ★★ **Hunterian Art Gallery.** A part of the University of Glasgow's Hunterian Museum, this is the oldest public museum in Scotland (opened in 1803). The gallery inherited the artistic estate of Scottish-American James McNeill Whistler (1834–1903) and many of his paintings hang here. You'll also find a selection of Scottish Colorists, as well as a collection of 17th- and 18th-century European masters (from Rembrandt to Rubens). One wing of the building has a re-creation of Charles Rennie Mackintosh's Glasgow home. ⏱ *1½ hr. University of Glasgow, 22 Hillhead*

The Hunterian Art Gallery is the oldest public museum in Scotland.

St. ☎ *0141/330-5431. www. hunterian.gla.ac.uk. Free admission (gallery), £3 (Mackintosh House). Mon–Sat 9:30am–5pm. Bus: 44. Underground: Hillhead.*

Giant chess game at the Science Museum.

Glasgow's **Best Architecture**

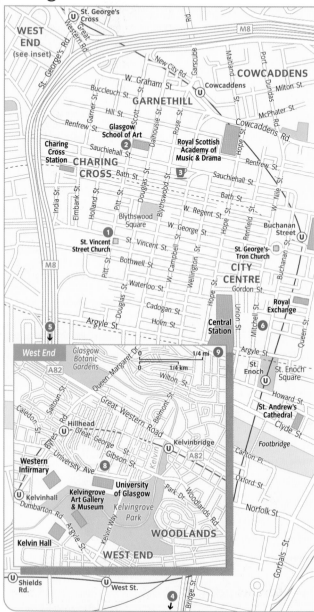

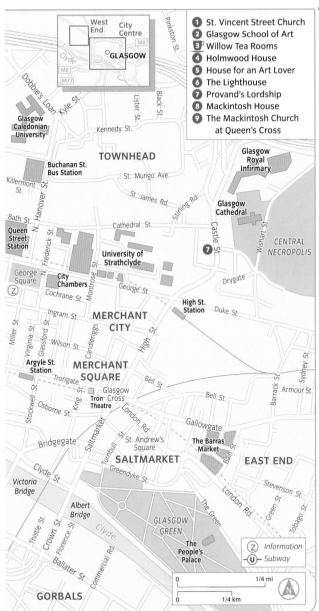

1 St. Vincent Street Church
2 Glasgow School of Art
3 Willow Tea Rooms
4 Holmwood House
5 House for an Art Lover
6 The Lighthouse
7 Provand's Lordship
8 Mackintosh House
9 The Mackintosh Church at Queen's Cross

West End
City Centre
M8
Clyde
GLASGOW
M8
M77

Pinkston St.

Black St.

Lister St.

Dobbie's Loan

Kyle St.

Kennedy St.

Glasgow Caledonian University

Killermont St.

Buchanan St. Bus Station

TOWNHEAD

St. Mungo Ave.

Glasgow Royal Infirmary

St. James Rd.

Stirling Rd.

Bath St.

N. Hanover St.

Queen Street Station

Frederick St.

Cathedral St.

Glasgow Cathedral

Castle St.

CENTRAL NECROPOLIS

Wishart St.

George Square

City Chambers

Z

University of Strathclyde

Montrose St.

George St.

7

Drygate

Cochrane St.

Ingram St.

MERCHANT CITY

High St. Station

Duke St.

Miller St.

Virginia St.

Glassford St.

Candleriggs

High St.

Wilson St.

Argyle St. Station

MERCHANT SQUARE

Bell St.

Bell St.

Sydney St.

Barrack St.

Armour St.

Stockwell St.

Osborne St.

Trongate

King St.

Saltmarket

Glasgow Cross

Tron Theatre

London Rd.

Gallowgate

Bridgegate

Turnbull St.

St. Andrew's Square

The Barras Market

Bain St.

EAST END

Clyde St.

SALTMARKET

Greendyke St.

London Rd.

Stevenson St.

Green St.

Tobago St.

Victoria Bridge

Albert Bridge

Thistle St.

Crown St.

Florence St.

Clyde

GLASGOW GREEN

The Green

Ballater St.

Commercial Rd.

The People's Palace

GORBALS

Z Information
U Subway

0   1/4 mi
0   1/4 km

N

Amazingly, after Glasgow survived the World War II bombing raids mostly intact, some city planners wanted to knock down all its surviving Victorian buildings for the sake of new development. Too much has been demolished, but the city remains a paragon of 19th-century architecture. This tour will give you the highlights, but just a stroll around the city center is an eye-opener.
START: **Take Bus 62 to St. Vincent Street Church at 265 St. Vincent St.**

St. Vincent Street Church is note-worthy for its Greek-influenced exterior.

❶ ★★ St. Vincent Street Church (Glasgow City Free Church).

Despite limited access, the building remains the most visible landmark attributed to one of the city's two greatest architects, Alexander 'Greek' Thomson (1817–75). Built in 1859, it runs counter to

The gift shop at the Glasgow School of Art.

the contemporary fashion of Gothic Revival. Two classic Greek porticos enclose a brilliant clock tower decorated in a unique and curiously sympathetic mix of Egyptian, Assyrian, and Indian-looking motifs. ⏲ *15 min. (unless attending services/tours arranged by appointment). 265 St. Vincent St. ☎ 0141/221-1937. www. greekthomsonchurch.com. Sunday services at 11am and 6pm.*

❷ ★★★ Glasgow School of Art.

This building, a blend of the Arts and Craft movement with Art Nouveau, was completed in 1909 and is one of Charles Rennie Mackintosh's masterpieces. Take the tour to see the interior details, such as the sun porch looking back over the city and what is the most impressive small library ever devised. In another room, there are some original watercolor paintings by the great architect. ⏲ *1½ hr. 167 Renfrew St. ☎ 0141/353-4526. www. gsa.ac.uk. Tours £8.75 adults, £7*

Afternoon tea at the Willow Tearooms.

students/seniors, £4 under 18s, £23.50 family. Tours Apr–mid May and mid-Sept–Oct daily 11am, 3pm, 5pm; Mid-May–mid-June GSA degree show (tour times vary); mid-June–mid-Sept hourly 10am–5pm; Nov–Feb 11am, 3pm. GSA shop: daily spring and autumn 10:30am–7pm, summer 9:30am–7pm, winter 10:30am–5pm. Underground: Cowcaddens.

Where else to get a cup of tea on this tour but the ③ **Willow Tea Rooms**. Designed by Mackintosh in 1904 for the infamous Kate Cranston—a temperance advocate and Mackintosh patron—some of the establishment's original features remain in the Room de Luxe. Afternoon tea starts at £12.50 per person. *217 Sauchiehall St.* ☎ *0141/332-0521. www.willowtearooms. co.uk. £.*

④ ★★★ **Holmwood House.** This villa, designed by Alexander Thomson and built in 1858, is probably the best example of his innovative style in Victorian homes. Magnificently original, its restoration (which is ongoing) has revealed that Thomson concerned himself with every detail, down to the wallpaper. Most impressive is the overall exterior design, and the interior parlor and the cornices in the dining room. ⏱ *1½ hr. 61–63 Netherlee Rd., Cathcart, about 6km (4 miles) south of the city center.* ☎ *0141/637-2129. www.nts.org.uk. Admission £6 adults; £5 student, seniors, and children; £15.50 family. Apr–Oct Thurs–Mon noon–5pm. Bus: 44 or 66. Train: Cathcart.*

⑤ **House for an Art Lover.** Mackintosh devotees flock here, but

Ahead of His Time: Charles Rennie Mackintosh

Although legendary today and his works recognized the world over, Charles Rennie Mackintosh (1868–1928) was largely forgotten in Scotland at the end of his life. Forms of nature, especially plants, inspired his elegant motifs, which were far from the fashion of the day. Most of his work is in Glasgow but about 40 kilometers (25 miles) west of Glasgow, in Helensburgh, is his greatest achievement in residential design: Hill House. For more information on all his buildings, visit the website of the **Charles Rennie Mackintosh Society** at www.crmsociety.com, or call ☎ 0141/946-6600.

Unappreciated Genius: Alexander 'Greek' Thomson

Perhaps even more important than Mackintosh, Alexander 'Greek' Thomson (1817–75) brought an unrivaled vision to Glasgow. While the influence of classical Greece was nothing new to Victorian architects, Thomson honed it to essentials and then mixed in Egyptian, Assyrian, and other Eastern-influenced motifs. Like Mackintosh, he increasingly found himself out of step with (and well ahead of) others. While a number of his structures have been tragically lost to the wrecker's ball, some key works remain: for example, terraced houses such as **Moray Place** (where he lived on the city's Southside) or **Eton Terrace** near Glasgow University campus (p 135, ❹).

this is only a 20th-century architect's interpretation of what Mackintosh had in mind. Built in the mid-1990s, the home was constructed using basic drawings that Mackintosh created for a 1901 architecture competition. 🕐 *1 hr. Bellahouston Park, 10 Dumbreck Rd.* ☎ *0141/353-4770.*

Holmwood House is the best example of Alexander Thomson's Victorian style.

www.houseforanartlover.co.uk. Admission £4.50 adults; £3 seniors, students, and children; £12 family. Apr–Sept Mon–Wed 10am–4pm, Thurs–Sat 10am–1pm; Oct–Mar Sat–Sun 10am–1pm (weekday times by arrangement). Bus: 3, 9, 54, or 55. Underground: Ibrox.

❻ **The Lighthouse.** This is Mackintosh's first public commission (in 1895), designed to be the HQ for the Glasgow Herald newspaper. In 2009, a decade after the building's relaunch as the center for design and architecture in Scotland, the management went into administration, although the city has tried to keep it going. 🕐 *15 min. 11 Mitchell Lane.* ☎ *0141/276-5365. www.the lighthouse.co.uk. Underground: St. Enoch.*

❼ ★ **Provand's Lordship.** Glasgow's oldest surviving house, built in the 1470s, is the only reminder of the clusters of medieval homes that once surrounded Glasgow Cathedral (St. Mungos). Thanks to the 17th-century furniture (from the original collection of Sir William Burrell), you get a feel for what the interiors once were like. The tiny doors are the best evidence of this building's true age. 🕐 *1 hr.*

The Lighthouse is the home of Scotland's Centre for Architecture and Design.

3 Castle St. ☎ 0141/552-8819. www.
glasgowmuseums.com. Free admission. Mon–Thurs, Sat 10am–5pm,
Fri, Sun 11am–5pm. Bus: 11, 36, 37,
38, 42, or 89. Train: High St.

❽ ★★ Mackintosh House. Part
of the Hunterian Art Gallery, this is a

A bedroom at Mackintosh House.

literal re-creation of Mackintosh's
Glasgow home from 1906 to 1914. It
covers three levels, decorated in the
original style of the famed architect
and his artist wife Margaret Macdonald. All salvageable fittings
and fixtures were recovered from
the original home before it was
demolished in the mid-1960s. *See
p 127,* **❺**.

**❾ ★ The Mackintosh Church
at Queen's Cross.** This restored
attraction entails a bit of a trek, but in
addition to showing off the architect's
penchant for simple beauty and his
timeless vision (the stained-glass windows are characteristic of his design
aesthetic), it is the official Mackintosh
Society's HQ, with a good resource
center and shop. The church, completed in 1899, is the only kirk ever
designed by Mackintosh that was
actually built. ⏱ *1 hr. 870 Garscube
Rd.* ☎ *0141/946-6600. www.crm
society.com. Admission £4 adults,
children free. Mar–Oct Mon, Wed,
and Fri 10am–5pm; Nov–Feb Mon
and Fri 10am–5pm. Bus: 40 or 61.*

A West End **Stroll**

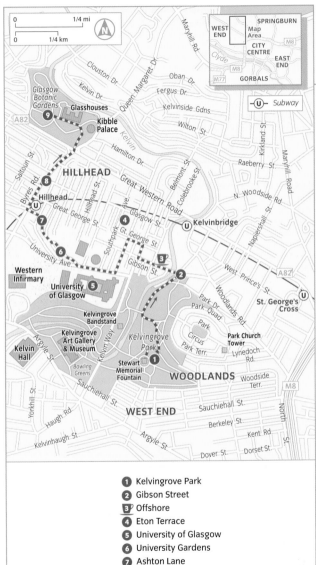

0   1/4 mi
0   1/4 km

SPRINGBURN
WEST END   Map Area
CITY CENTRE
EAST END
GORBALS

—U— Subway

Glasgow Botanic Gardens
9 Glasshouses
Kibble Palace

HILLHEAD

8 Byres Rd
Hillhead —U—
7
6 University Ave.

Great Western Road

4 Glasgow St. —U— **Kelvinbridge**
Gt. George St.
Gibson St. **3**
2

St. George's Cross —U—

Western Infirmary
5 University of Glasgow

Kelvingrove Bandstand
Kelvingrove Art Gallery & Museum
Kelvin Hall
Bowling Greens
Kelvingrove Park
Stewart Memorial Fountain **1**

Park Church Tower

WOODLANDS

WEST END
Sauchiehall St.
Berkeley St.
Argyle St.

1. Kelvingrove Park
2. Gibson Street
3. Offshore
4. Eton Terrace
5. University of Glasgow
6. University Gardens
7. Ashton Lane
8. Byres Road
9. Botanic Gardens

This walk will take you through the leafy and trendy West End. The area's urban development began in the 19th century as Glasgow, a booming center for manufacturing, needed more space to house its ever-growing population; it soon became the Second City of the British Empire—in both number of residents and industrial might. START: **take bus 9, 16, 18, 18A, 42, or 62 to Kelvingrove Art Gallery and Museum.**

The Gothic Stewart Memorial Fountain in Kelvingrove Park.

1 ★★ Kelvingrove Park. This hilly park on the banks of the River Kelvin was commissioned by Sir Joseph Paxton in 1854. One popular meeting spot, particularly on sunny days, is the **Gothic Stewart Memorial Fountain** (honoring Robert Stewart, the lord provost who helped supply the city with drinking water). The fountain is ornamented with signs of the Zodiac and scenes that depict the source of the city's main supply of water, Loch Katrine. ⏱ *30 min. Free admission. Daily dawn–dusk.*

Exit the park on to:

2 Gibson Street. One of the calmer commercial streets in the West End, with a good selection of cafe/bars and restaurants. You're now inside the Hillhead district, which encompasses the main campus of the University of Glasgow on Gilmorehill and the Western Infirmary. ⏱ *10 min.*

3 ◗ Offshore is a laidback cafe with welcoming sofas, and an ideal spot to stop for a cappuccino, herbal tea, or a light meal (usually for less than a fiver). *3–5 Gibson St. No phone. From Eldon St. to Oakfield Ave. £.*

4 ★ Eton Terrace. The unmistakable hand of architect Alexander Thomson is apparent on this row of houses, completed in 1864. Note

Annual International Events

Glasgow hosts some annual festivals that essentially hold their own against Edinburgh's better-known summer options. **★★ Celtic Connections** (☎ 0141/353-8000; www.celticconnections.com) is the best-attended annual festival in Glasgow, and the largest folk/traditional music festival of its kind in the world. It kicks off the year every January. The **Glasgow Film Festival** (☎ 0141/332-6535; www.glasgowfilmfestival.org.uk) gets better every year, screening more than 100 movies in mid-February. Finally, a lone piper can sound impressive; a band-full of bagpipes blown in unison, however, is one of the most stirring sounds on the planet. Every August, at **Piping Live!** (☎ 0141/353-8000; www.pipingfestival.co.uk), the cream of the crop of international piping ensembles congregate in Glasgow.

the two temple-like facades serving as bookends; their double porches are fashioned after the Choragic Monument of *Thrasyllus* in Athens. For all his admiration of Eastern design, it is surprising to know that Thomson never traveled outside the UK. 🕑 *15 min. Oakfield Ave., off Great George St.*

No. 12, University Gardens was built by architect J. Gaff Gillespie.

⑤ ★★ University of Glasgow. Founded in 1451, the university moved to its current location in the 1860s. English architect Sir George Gilbert Scott (1811–78), who designed London's Albert Memorial, completed the campus's Gothic Revival main building, punctuated by a 30m (98-ft.) tower—a virtual beacon on the horizon of the West End. Between the two central quadrangles are cloistered vaults, evoking a sense of meditation and reflection. 🕑 *20 min. University Ave. www.gla.ac.uk.*

⑥ ★ University Gardens. This fine street of houses was designed primarily by Scottish architect J. J. Burnet (1857–1938) in the 1880s. Take a moment to admire No. 12, built by architect J. Gaff Gillespie in 1900-classic 'Glasgow Style', with Mackintosh and Art Nouveau influences. 🕑 *20 min.*

⑦ ★ Ashton Lane. This cobbled mews is the heart of the West End's nightlife, although it bustles right through the day too. Its host of bars, cafes, and restaurants includes the venerable **Ubiquitous**

A greenhouse at the Botanic Gardens.

Chip (see p 144), which is located in a building that once functioned as the stables for an undertaker. ⏱ *15 min.*

8 ★★ **Byres Road.** The proverbial Main Street of the West End,

People sitting outside one of many cafes on Byres Road.

Byres Road is chockablock with pubs and bars, cafes and restaurants, and lots of shops. If you're interested in antiques and vintage clothing, detour down Ruthven Lane. Look up as you approach Dowanside Road to note the **Victoria Cross** sign; it's a remnant of a time when an attempt—derailed by locals—was made to change the name of the Byres Road to Victoria Road. ⏱ *1 hr. From University Ave. to Great Western Rd. www.byres-road.co.uk.*

9 ★ **Botanic Gardens.** On dour days, Kibble Palace—a domed, cast-iron-and-glass greenhouse with exotic plants—is a welcome escape. Greenhouses at the gardens contain orchid and cactus collections, while the outdoor attractions include a working vegetable plot, a rose garden, and a 200-year-old weeping ash. ⏱ *1 hr. 730 Great Western Rd. (at Queen Margaret Dr.).*

Dining in Glasgow

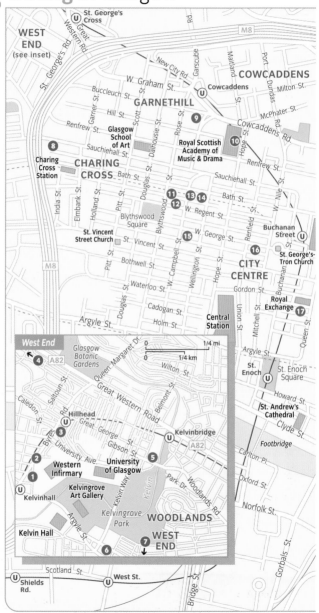

WEST END (see inset)

St. George's Cross

COWCADDENS

Cowcaddens

GARNETHILL

W. Graham St.

Buccleuch St.

Hill St.

Renfrew St.

Glasgow School of Art

McPhater St.

Cowcaddens Rd.

Royal Scottish Academy of Music & Drama

Renfrew St.

Charing Cross Station

Sauchiehall St.

CHARING CROSS

Bath St.

Sauchiehall St.

Bath St.

Blythswood Square

W. Regent St.

St. Vincent Street Church

St. Vincent St.

W. George St.

Buchanan Street

Bothwell St.

W. George St.

CITY CENTRE

St. George's-Tron Church

Waterloo St.

Cadogan St.

Gordon St.

Royal Exchange

Holm St.

Central Station

Argyle St.

Argyle St.

West End

Glasgow Botanic Gardens

0   1/4 mi
0   1/4 km

Wilton St.

St. Enoch

St. Enoch Square

Howard St.

Great Western Road

Hillhead

Great George St.

Gibson St.

Kelvinbridge

St. Andrew's Cathedral

Clyde St.

University of Glasgow

Footbridge

Western Infirmary

Carlton Pl.

Kelvingrove Art Gallery

Oxford St.

Kelvinhall

Kelvingrove Park

WOODLANDS

Norfolk St.

Kelvin Hall

WEST END

Scotland St.

West St.

Shields Rd.

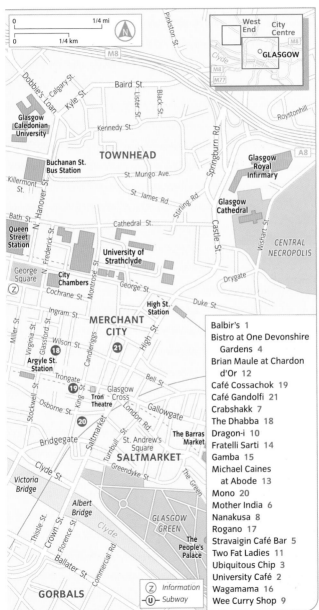

Balbir's 1
Bistro at One Devonshire Gardens 4
Brian Maule at Chardon d'Or 12
Café Cossachok 19
Café Gandolfi 21
Crabshakk 7
The Dhabba 18
Dragon-i 10
Fratelli Sarti 14
Gamba 15
Michael Caines at Abode 13
Mono 20
Mother India 6
Nanakusa 8
Rogano 17
Stravaigin Café Bar 5
Two Fat Ladies 11
Ubiquitous Chip 3
University Café 2
Wagamama 16
Wee Curry Shop 9

Dining Best Bets

Outside dining at the Ubiquitous Chip.

Best Fish & Seafood
★★★ Gamba, *225a W. George St. (p 142)*

Best Entertainment
★ Café Cossachok, *38 Albion St. (p 141)*

Best Brasserie
★★ Café Gandolfi, *64 Albion St. (p 141)*

Best Indian
★★ The Dhabba, *44 Candleriggs (p 141)*

Best Chinese
★ Dragon-i, *313 Hope St. (p 141)*

Best Pizza
★ Fratelli Sarti, *133 Wellington St. (p 142)*

Best Fancy French
★ Michael Caines at Abode, *129 Bath St. (p 142)*

Best Neighborhood Restaurant
★ Two Fat Ladies, *88 Dumbarton Rd. (p 144)*

Best Art Deco Design
★ Rogano, *11 Exchange Place (p 143)*

Best Landmark Restaurant
★★ Ubiquitous Chip, *12 Ashton Lane (p 144)*

Best for Families
★ Wagamama, *97–103 W. George St. (p 144)*

Best Cheap Eats
★★ Wee Curry Shop, *7 Buccleuch St. (p 144)*

Best Gastro-Pub
★ Stravaigin Café Bar, *28 Gibson St. (p 143)*

Glasgow Dining A to Z

★ **Balbir's** WEST END *INDIAN* A sprawling restaurant, serving up first-class Indian specialties. The tandoori oven is used to good effect, especially on the appetizer of barbequed salmon. *7 Church St.* ☎ *0141/339-7711. www.balbirs restaurants.co.uk. Main courses £8–£14. AE, MC, V. Dinner daily. Underground: Kelvinhall.*

★★ **Bistro at One Devonshire Gardens** WEST END *FRENCH/MODERN SCOTTISH* Based in a top hotel (p 150), this sumptuous restaurant aspires to be number one in the city too. The menu changes frequently and encompasses everything from Pacific oysters to aged steaks. *Hotel du Vin at One Devonshire Gardens, 1 Devonshire Gardens* ☎ *0141/339-2001. www.hotelduvin.com. Main courses £20–£25. AE, MC, V. Lunch & dinner daily. Bus: 9, 20, or 66.*

★ **Brian Maule at Chardon d'Or** COMMERCIAL CENTER *FRENCH/MODERN SCOTTISH* Maule cut his teeth at some of the best restaurants in France and London before returning to his home, Scotland. Expect to sample the likes of roast Guinea fowl or braised cheek of Scotch beef with wild mushroom

ragout. *176 West Regent St.* ☎ *0141/ 248-3801. www.brianmaule.com. Main courses £23–£27. AE, MC, V. Dinner daily, lunch Mon–Fri. Underground: Buchanan St.*

★ **Café Cossachok** MERCHANT CITY *RUSSIAN* A restaurant that mixes a gallery/performance space with food on a hearty Slavic/Russian theme. Come here for borscht soup or blinis, and then stick around for some live music (the owner is a professional violinist). *10 King St.* ☎ *0141/553-0733. www.cossachok. com. Main courses £9–£15. MC, V. Lunch Tues–Thurs, dinner Tues–Sun. Underground: St. Enoch.*

★★ **Café Gandolfi** MERCHANT CITY *BISTRO* This favorite of local foodies serves up solid cooking at the right price. Particularly recommended are the Stornoway black pudding and creamy Cullen skink (smoked haddock chowder). *64 Albion St.* ☎ *0141/ 552-6813. www.cafegandolfi.com. Main courses £8–£14. MC, V. Breakfast Mon–Sat, lunch & dinner daily. Underground: Buchanan St.*

Crabshakk WEST END *FISH/SEAFOOD* The menu here varies from moderately priced fish dishes, such

Bistro at One Devonshire Gardens.

Fratelli Sarti for pizza and Italian coffee.

as smoked mackerel with horserad-ish or a fish club sandwich served with chips, to more pricey whole crab or lobster. Generally, fish is only available if found fresh in the market that week. *1114 Argyle St.* ☎ *0141/334-6127. www.crabshakk. com. Main courses £7–£17. MC, V. Lunch & dinner Tues–Sun noon–6pm. Underground: Kelvinhall. Bus: 62. Map p 138.*

★★ **The Dhabba** MERCHANT CITY *INDIAN* A stylishly decorated

restaurant that specializes in North Indian cuisine. You may find it slightly more expensive than the average Glasgow curry house, but the refined ambience and flavors warrant it. *44 Candleriggs.* ☎ *0141/ 553-1249. www.thedhabba.com. Main courses £10–£18. AE, MC, V. Lunch & dinner daily. Underground: St. Enoch.*

★ **Dragon-i** COMMERCIAL CENTER *CHINESE* At the elegant Dragon-i, the cuisine is never boring or bland. Expect an excellent wine list and unusual dishes, such as tiger prawns with asparagus in a garlic chardonnay sauce. *313 Hope St.* ☎ *0141/332-7728. www.dragon-i. co.uk. Main courses £12.50–£16. AE, MC, V. Lunch Mon–Sat, dinner daily. Underground: Cowcaddens.*

★ kids **Fratelli Sarti** COMMER-CIAL CENTER *ITALIAN* The pizza at this cafe/deli is superb, with a thin, crispy crust and a perfect amount of topping. Alternatively, the 'al forno' pasta with sausage provides a satis-fying meal. Reservations are always advisable. *133 Wellington St.* ☎ *0141/248-2228. www.sarti.co.uk. Main courses £7–£10. AE, MC, V. Breakfast, lunch & dinner Mon–Sat;*

Beautifully displayed fish dish at Gamba.

Michael Caine's at ABode.

lunch & dinner Sun. Underground: Buchanan St.

★★★ **Gamba** COMMERCIAL CEN-TER *FISH/SEAFOOD*   This is the place to come for a first-rate fish dinner, often cooked using sustainable produce. Main courses may include North Atlantic cod with prawn and caper or seared hand-dived scallops with chorizo and apple salad. *225a W. George St.* ☎ *0141/572-0899. www.gamba. co.uk. Main courses £19–£26. AE, MC, V. Dinner daily, lunch Mon–Sat. Underground: Buchanan St.*

★ **Michael Caines at ABode** COMMERCIAL CENTER *FRENCH*   It's hard to find fault with the cooking and presentation at this chic hotel restaurant. Dishes on the regularly changing menu might include Goosnargh duck with scotch egg and fig purée or a honey bavarois dessert. *129 Bath St. (in the ABode hotel).* ☎ *0141/221-6789. www.michael caines.com. Main courses £20–£27; 7-course tasting menu £68. AE, MC, V. Lunch & dinner Mon–Sat. Underground: Buchanan St.*

Mono MERCHANT CITY *VEGAN* This hip and welcoming bar/diner serves internationally inspired vegetarian and vegan-friendly meals in laid-back surroundings. Mono also houses a CD shop, literally next to the bar, with the latest in indie rock. *12 Kings Court.* ☎ *0141/553-2400. www.monocafebar.com. Main courses £6.50–£7.50. AE, MC, V. Lunch & dinner daily. Underground: St. Enoch.*

★★ **Mother India** WEST END *INDIAN*   In business for more than a decade, this is the most respected Indian restaurant in Glasgow. The menu is not overloaded with too many dishes, and the staff is attentive. Down the road, a second branch—Mother India's Café—offers less expensive, tapas-style dishes. *28 Westminster Terrace (at Kelvingrove St.).* ☎ *0141/221-1663. www.motherindia.co.uk. Main courses £9–£14. MC, V. Dinner daily, lunch Wed–Sat. Bus: 16, 18, or 42.*

★ **Nanakusa** COMMERCIAL CENTER *JAPANESE*   This restaurant covers a wide selection of Japanese cuisine, from sushi and sashimi to teppanyaki and tempura; not to mention bento boxes, rice dishes, side plates such as gyoza, and big steamy, slurpy noodle bowls. It's casual yet stylish. *441 Sauchiehall St.* ☎ *0141/332-6303. Main courses £7–£10 . MC, V. Dinner daily, lunch Mon–Sat. Train: Charing Cross. Map p 138.*

★ **Rogano** COMMERCIAL CENTER *FISH/SEAFOOD* This landmark and celebrity favorite (the oldest continually operating restaurant in the city) has a well-preserved Art Deco interior patterned after the Queen Mary ocean liner. The look is sometimes more impressive than the traditional cuisine. But go for champagne and oysters if nothing else and soak up the 1930s charm. *11 Exchange Place.* ☎ *0141/248-4055. www.roganoglasgow.com. Main courses £23–£40. AE, DC, MC, V. Lunch & dinner daily. Underground: Buchanan St.*

★ **Stravaigin Café Bar** WEST END *MODERN SCOTTISH* The motto here is 'think global, eat local.' Scottish produce receives an international twist, with dishes like cheese and herb fritters with sweet chili sauce and Arbroath smokie stuffed with rice. *28 Gibson St.* ☎ *0141/334-2665. www.stravaigin. com. Main courses £6–£10. AE, MC, V. Lunch & dinner daily. Underground: Kelvinbridge.*

★ **Two Fat Ladies** COMMERCIAL CENTER *SCOTTISH/FISH* A casual bistro whose specialties include oven-baked halibut, fish platter, or black-olive-stuffed chicken. In addition to the smart, shiny bistro in the city center, there are two other branches in the West End. *118a Blythswood St.* ☎ *0141/847-0088. www.twofatladiesrestaurant.com Main courses £16–£18. MC, V. Lunch & dinner daily. Underground: Buchanan St.*

★★ **Ubiquitous Chip** WEST END *MODERN SCOTTISH* No restaurant has been more responsible for a culinary renaissance in Scotland than this place, set inside the walls of a former stable. The ever-changing menu might feature haunch of Galloway roe deer, poached wild seabass, or West Coast langoustines. *12 Ashton Lane (near Byres Rd.).* ☎ *0141/334-5007. www. ubiquitouschip.co.uk. Reservations recommended. Set dinner £40. AE, DC, MC, V. Lunch & dinner daily. Underground: Hillhead.*

kids **University Café** WEST END *CAFE* The 'Knickerbocker Glory' is the king of the ice-cream sundae in Scotland, and few places do it better than this Art Deco landmark with all original features from booths to counters. Comfort foods, macaroni cheese, and fish suppers also feature. *87 Byres Rd.* ☎ *0141/339-5217. Main courses £6–£10. No credit cards. Daily 9am to 10pm. Underground: Hillhead. Map p 138.*

Fabulous shellfish at Two Fat Ladies.

The Ubiquitous Chip is housed in a former stable.

★ kids **Wagamama** COMMERCIAL CENTER *JAPANESE* This chain of casual noodle bars has proved successful in Glasgow. Seating is at long tables and benches, and service is fast and efficient. It's one of the best places in town for a quick bite and is very child-friendly. *97–103 W. George St. ☎ 0141/229-1468. www. wagamama.com. Main courses £6.50–£10. MC, V. Lunch & dinner daily. Underground: Buchanan St.*

★★ **Wee Curry Shop** COMMERCIAL CENTER *INDIAN* This tiny place offers the best low-cost Indian dishes in the city. The menu is concise but perfectly sufficient, with dishes such as green herb vegetable pakora. Two other branches are in the West End. *7 Buccleuch St. ☎ 0141/353-0777. www.weecurryshopglasgow.co.uk. Main courses £6–£10. No credit cards. Lunch Mon–Sat, dinner daily. Underground: Cowcaddens.*

Food & Wine on the Run

Glasgow rather excels in its modern delicatessens. Heart **Buchanan Fine Food and Wine** (380 Byres Rd., ☎ 0141/334-7626) is perfect for picnic nosh to take to the nearby Botanic Gardens. If you're a cheese lover, then a stop by the tiny ★★ **IJ Mellis Cheesemonger** (492 Great Western Rd., ☎ 0141/339-8998) is necessary for an outstanding selection of British and Irish cheeses. Nearby is the Glasgow branch of **Lupe Pintos,** (313 Great Western Rd., ☎ 0141/334-5444): It's the perfect stop for Mexican and American foodstuffs.

Peckham's has several branches. If you're on the east side of the city center, their merchant city shop (61 Glassford St., ☎ 0141/553-0666) offers a full delicatessen with fresh bread and a good wine shop in the basement. On Glasgow's Southside, in the Shawlands district near Queens Park, the **1901 Deli** (11 Skirving St., ☎ 0141/632-1630) has a plentiful supply of treats for any outdoor feast.

Hotels in Glasgow

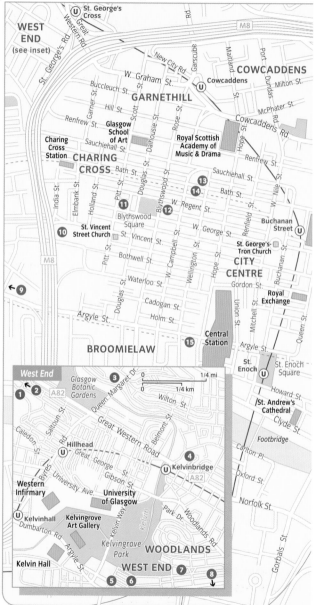

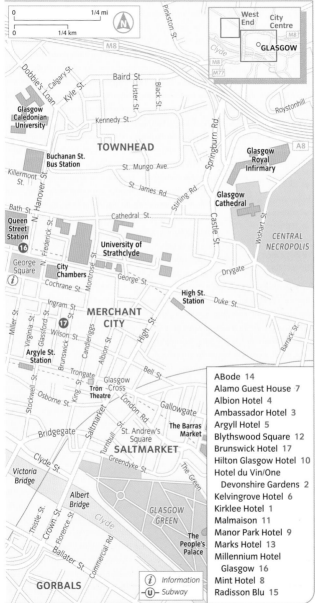

ABode 14
Alamo Guest House 7
Albion Hotel 4
Ambassador Hotel 3
Argyll Hotel 5
Blythswood Square 12
Brunswick Hotel 17
Hilton Glasgow Hotel 10
Hotel du Vin/One
  Devonshire Gardens 2
Kelvingrove Hotel 6
Kirklee Hotel 1
Malmaison 11
Manor Park Hotel 9
Marks Hotel 13
Millennium Hotel
  Glasgow 16
Mint Hotel 8
Radisson Blu 15

Hotel Best Bets

Most Glamorous Hotel
★★★ Hotel du Vin/One Devonshire Gardens, *1 Devonshire Gardens (p 150)*

Best Small Hotel
★ Ambassador Hotel, *7 Kelvin Dr.
(p 149)*

Best Hip Hotel
★ Brunswick Hotel, *106–108 Brunswick St. (p 149)*

Best Family Hotel
Kirklee Hotel, *11 Kensington Gate
(p 150)*

Best Boutique Hotel
★ Malmaison, *278 W. George St.
(p 150)*

Best Guesthouse
★★ Alamo Guest House, *46 Gray
St. (p 149)*

Best Traditional Hotel
★ Hilton Glasgow Hotel, *1 William
St. (p 150)*

Most Central Hotel
Millennium Hotel Glasgow, *George
Sq. (p 151)*

Best Highland Lodge Style
★ Manor Park Hotel, *28 Balshagray
Dr. (p 150)*

Best River Views
Mint Hotel, *Finnieston Quay (p 151)*

Best Hotel Spa Facilities
★★ Blythswood Square, *11 Blythswood Sq. (p 149)*

Best Large Modern Hotel
★ Radisson Blu, *301 Argyle St.
(p 151)*

The Hilton Glasgow is the city's best traditional hotel.

ABode COMMERCIAL CENTER Formerly the Arthouse Hotel, this handsome Edwardian building is now a striking boutique offering. Colors and textures blend in with the older structure, while the commissioned art and period pieces evoke some of the original splendor. *129 Bath St.* ☎ *0141/221-6789. www.abodehotels.co.uk/glagsow. 65 units. Doubles from £165. AE, DC, MC, V. Underground: Buchanan St.*

★★ **Alamo Guest House** WEST END A highly regarded hotel that faces onto a corner of Kelvingrove Park, with many of its Victorian flourishes intact. The only downside is that most of the beautifully dressed rooms do not have ensuite private bathrooms. *46 Gray St.* ☎ *0141/339-2395. www.alamo guesthouse.com. 12 units. Double £66–£155. MC, V. Underground: Kelvinhall. Map p 146.*

Albion Hotel WEST END This unpretentious and friendly hotel occupies two nearly identical sandstone row houses in a convenient and leafy district of the West End. Its high-ceilinged units have modern furniture and shower-only bathrooms. *405–407 N. Woodside Rd.* ☎ *0141/339-8620. www.glasgow hotelsandapartments.co.uk. 20 units. Doubles £70. AE, DC, MC, V. Underground: Kelvin Bridge.*

★ **Ambassador Hotel** WEST END Across from the Botanic Gardens, this small Edwardian townhouse (part of the same hotel group that runs the Albion) offers recently refurbished and modern bedrooms, with ensuite bathrooms (some with bath tubs). *7 Kelvin Dr.* ☎ *0141/946-1018. www.glasgowhotelsandapartments. co.uk. 16 units. Doubles £70. AE, DC, MC, V. Underground: Hillhead.*

Argyll Hotel WEST END Only a short walk from Kelvingrove Park, the Argyll lives up to its Scottish name. The atmosphere here is more Highland lodge than urban inn, with an understated and tasteful use of tartan in its furnishings. There is a clutch of spacious family rooms. *969–973 Sauchiehall St.* ☎ *0141/ 337-3313. www.argyllhotelglasgow. co.uk. 38 units. Doubles £90. AE, MC, V. Underground: Kelvin Hall.*

★★ **Blythswood Square** COMMERICAL CENTER This is a recent addition to the higher end of the city's hotel market. The rooms are often spacious with black granite bathrooms, whilst the basement spa is a labyrinth of massage rooms, saunas, whirlpool baths, steam rooms, and a relaxation pool. *11 Blythswood Sq.* ☎ *0141/208-2458. www.townhousecompany.com/ blythswoodsquare. 100 units. Doubles £120–£245. AE, MC, V. Underground: Buchanan St.*

★ **Brunswick Hotel** MERCHANT CITY One of the hippest hotels in town, though it's far from pretentious. The units are generally small but soothing and inviting, with neutral

Hip yet unpretentious styling at the Brunswick.

color schemes, comfortable mattresses, and adequate bathrooms (several with both tub and shower). *106–108 Brunswick St.* ☎ *0141/552-0001. www.brunswickhotel.co.uk. 18 units. Doubles £85–£100. AE, DC, MC, V. Underground: Buchanan St.*

★ kids Hilton Glasgow Hotel

COMMERCIAL CENTER Glasgow's first-class Hilton is perched over the M8 freeway that slashes through the city of Glasgow. Despite its odd location, it is a classy and modern hotel, with plush but conservative units that offer good city views. *1 William St.* ☎ *800/445-8667 in the US and Canada, or 0141/204-5555. www. hilton.co.uk/glasgow. 331 units. Doubles £100–£180. AE, DC, MC, V. Suburban train: Charing Cross.*

★★★ Hotel du Vin/One Devonshire Gardens

WEST END This luxurious boutique hotel, spread over five townhouses, is the most glamorous the city has to offer—often favored by the rich and famous. The guest rooms have all the necessary modern gadgets, and the hotel's Bistro offers first-class dining (see p 141). *1 Devonshire Gardens* ☎ *0141/339-2001. www. hotelduvin.com. 49 units. Doubles from £145. AE, DC, MC, V. Underground: Hillhead.*

Hotel du Vin/One Devonshire Gardens is Glasgows most glamorous hotel.

Chic bedroom at Malmaison.

★ Kelvingrove Hotel

WEST END Now part of the McQuade Group, this small guesthouse offers comfortable accommodation with modern decor, set within converted flats. Particularly favorable for its location near Kelvingrove Park and for the top-notch personal service from staff. *944 Sauchiehall St.* ☎ *0141/339-5011. www.kelvingrove-hotel.co.uk. 22 units. Doubles £60. MC, V. Bus: 16, 18A, or 42A.*

kids Kirklee Hotel

WEST END A red-sandstone Edwardian terraced house, with elegant bay windows, overlooking a private garden. A few of the high-ceilinged bedrooms are large enough to accommodate families. *11 Kensington Gate.* ☎ *0141/334-5555. www.kirkleehotel.co.uk. 9 units. Doubles £75, family £85–£100. MC, V. Underground: Hillhead.*

★ Malmaison

COMMERCIAL CENTER The decor of this converted church, with its fine Greek-style exterior, is sleek and contemporary. Units vary in size from quite cozy to average, but all are chic and well appointed. Larger rooms are in the original church conversion, but access there is by stairs only. *278 W. George St.* ☎ *0141/572-1000. www.malmaison-glasgow.com. 72 units. Doubles £140. AE, DC, MC, V. Suburban train: Charing Cross.*

★ Manor Park Hotel

WEST END Slightly off the beaten track, this Highlands-themed townhouse (built

No Frills in the City Centre

For basic and inexpensive overnight rooms, Glasgow has a few options. Near Sauchiehall Street, the **Hotel Ibis** (220 West Regent St. ☎ 0141/225-6000, www.ibishotel.com) is well-located and has rooms starting around £60. In the New Gorbals, on the south bank of the River Clyde, the **Premier Inn** (80 Ballater St. ☎ 0870/243-6452, www.premierinn.com) also has doubles from £60. Opened in 2007, the **Etap Hotel,** also south of the river, has become popular for those on a budget who are satisfied with basic, clean accommodation (Springfield Quay, ☎ 0141/429-8013, www.etaphotel.com).

in 1895, but first used as a hotel in 1947) offers traditionally furnished rooms, some with four poster beds. *28 Balshagray Dr. ☎ 0141/339-2143. www.manorparkhotel.com. 9 units. Doubles from £65. AE, DC, MC, V. Bus: 44 or 16.*

Marks Hotel COMMERCIAL CENTER   A bright and welcoming style-hotel with an enviable city center location. For quieter rooms, ask for those at the rear—though the front ones do have huge floor to ceiling windows that angle out over the street below. *110 Bath St. ☎ 0141/353-0800. www.markshotel.com. 103 units. Doubles £80–£225. AE, MC, V. Underground: Buchanan St. Map p 146.*

Millennium Hotel Glasgow COMMERCIAL CENTER   This landmark hotel, once called the Copthorne and erected at the beginning of the 19th century, has been thoroughly modernized. It faces onto the city's central plaza, George Square, and rooms in the front offer views of the opulent Glasgow city chambers. *George Sq. (at George St.). ☎ 0141/332-6711. www.millenniumhotels.com. 117 units. Doubles from £100. AE, DC, MC, V. Underground: Buchanan St.*

Mint Hotel WEST END   Located on the River Clyde, this smart hotel

with a waterside terrace is part of a small chain. All rooms feature fresh decor and are kitted out with Apple i-macs (with free, high-speed Wi-Fi) and power showers in the bathrooms. *Finnieston Quay. ☎ 0141/240-1002. www.minthotel.com. 164 units. Doubles £104. AE, DC, MC, V. Suburban train: Exhibition Centre.*

★ **Radisson Blu** COMMERCIAL CENTER   Still shiny since its November 2002 opening, the Radisson is just a stone's throw from Central Station. The contemporary guest rooms, with their blonde wood details and Scandinavian cool, have all the modern conveniences. *301 Argyle St. ☎ 0141/204-3333. www.radissonblu.co.uk/hotel-glasgow. 250 units. Doubles from £115. AE, DC, MC, V. Underground: St. Enoch.*

The ultramodern lobby bar of Radisson Blu.

Shopping in Glasgow

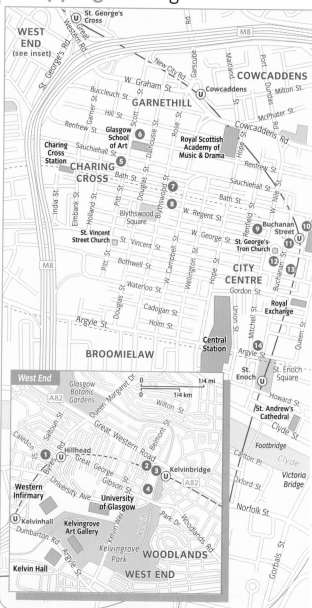

WEST
END
(see inset)

St. George's
Cross

COWCADDENS

Cowcaddens

GARNETHILL

Glasgow
School
of Art

Royal Scottish
Academy of
Music & Drama

Charing
Cross
Station

CHARING
CROSS

St. Vincent
Street Church

Blythswood
Square

Buchanan
Street

St. George's-
Tron Church

CITY
CENTRE

Royal
Exchange

BROOMIELAW

Central
Station

St.
Enoch

St. Enoch
Square

St. Andrew's
Cathedral

Footbridge

Victoria
Bridge

West End

Glasgow
Botanic
Gardens

Hillhead

Great Western Road

Kelvinbridge

Western
Infirmary

University
of Glasgow

Kelvinhall

Kelvingrove
Art Gallery

Kelvingrove
Park

Kelvin Hall

WOODLANDS

WEST END

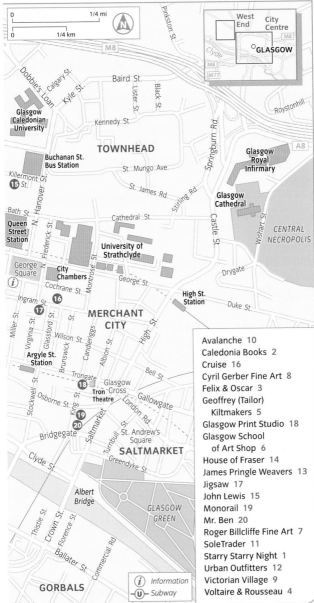

0   1/4 mi
0   1/4 km

West End
City Centre
GLASGOW

Pinkston St.

M8

Clyde
M8
M77

Dobbie's Loan
Calgary St.
Kyle St.
Baird St.
Lister St.
Black St.
Glasgow Caledonian University
Kennedy St.
Roystonhill
A8

TOWNHEAD

Buchanan St. Bus Station
St. Mungo Ave.
Springburn Rd.
Glasgow Royal Infirmary

Killermont St.
15
St. James Rd.
Stirling Rd.
Glasgow Cathedral

Bath St.
Hanover St.
Frederick St.
Cathedral St.
Castle St.
Wishart St.
CENTRAL NECROPOLIS

Queen Street Station
N.

George Square
City Chambers
University of Strathclyde
Montrose St.
George St.
Drygate

Ingram St.
17
Cochrane St.
16
High St. Station
Duke St.

Miller St.
Virginia St.
Glassford St.
MERCHANT CITY
High St.

Argyle St. Station
Brunswick St.
Albion St.
Wilson St.
Candleriggs
Bell St.

Stockwell St.
Osborne St.
Trongate
King St.
Glasgow Cross
Tron Theatre
18
Gallowgate
London Rd.

Bridgegate
19
20
Saltmarket
Turnbull St.
St. Andrew's Square
SALTMARKET

Clyde St.
Bridgegate
Greendyke St.

Albert Bridge
GLASGOW GREEN

Thistle St.
Crown St.
Florence St.
Ballater St.
Commercial Rd.

GORBALS

ⓘ Information
Ⓤ Subway

Avalanche 10
Caledonia Books 2
Cruise 16
Cyril Gerber Fine Art 8
Felix & Oscar 3
Geoffrey (Tailor) Kiltmakers 5
Glasgow Print Studio 18
Glasgow School of Art Shop 6
House of Fraser 14
James Pringle Weavers 13
Jigsaw 17
John Lewis 15
Monorail 19
Mr. Ben 20
Roger Billcliffe Fine Art 7
SoleTrader 11
Starry Starry Night 1
Urban Outfitters 12
Victorian Village 9
Voltaire & Rousseau 4

Shopping Best Bets

Heart Buchanan Fine Food and Wine.

Best Art Shop
★ Roger Billcliffe Fine Art, *134 Blythswood St. (p 155)*

Best Secondhand Books
★ Caledonia Books, *483 Great Western Rd. (p 155)*

Best Designer Labels
★ Cruise, *180 Ingram St. (p 155)*

Best Department Store
★ John Lewis, Buchanan Galleries *220 Buchanan St. (p 156)*

Best Food Shop
★★ Heart Buchanan Fine Food and Wine, *380 Byres Rd. (p 145)*

Best for Quirky Gifts
★★ Felix & Oscar, *459 Great Western Rd. (p 156)*

Best for Mackintosh Memorabilia
★ Glasgow School of Art Shop, *167 Renfrew St. (p 157)*

Best Alternative Music
★★ Monorail, *10 King St. (p 157)*

Best for Vintage
★ Mr. Ben, *101 King St. (p 156)*

Capital of Retail Therapy

Glasgow is the retail-therapy Mecca of Scotland, drawing customers from across the country. Shops are generally open 9am to 6pm, except Thursday, when they're open until 8pm, and Sunday, when they may open later and close earlier. Unless otherwise stated, all shops in the Commercial Center are best reached by the Underground station at Buchanan Street, which is the city's foremost shopping avenue.

Glasgow Shopping A to Z

Antiques

Victorian Village COMMERCIAL CENTER   This warren of shops offers a pleasantly claustrophobic clutter of goods. Some of the merchandise isn't particularly noteworthy, but there are some worthwhile pieces if you know what you're after and are willing to go hunting. *93 W. Regent St.* ☎ *0141/332-0808. MC, V. Underground: Buchanan St.*

Art

Cyril Gerber Fine Art COMMERICAL CENTER   One of Glasgow's best small galleries, it veers away from the avant-garde, specializing in British paintings of the 19th and 20th centuries. *148 W. Regent St.* ☎ *0141/221-3095. www.gerber fineart.co.uk. MC, V. Underground: Buchanan St.*

★★ Glasgow Print Studio MERCHANT CITY   In new premises as part of the uber-cool Trongate 103 art center, GPS sells limited edition etchings, wood blocks, aquatints, or screen prints. Good prices and a framing facility is on the premises.

Roger Bilcliffe Fine Art sells quality works by British artists.

97–101 Trongate. ☎ *0141/552-0704. www.gpsart.co.uk. MC, V. Bus: 66.*

★ Roger Billcliffe Fine Art COMMERCIAL CENTER   Fine artworks, from original contemporary paintings by British artists to delicate ceramics, are exhibited across several floors. *134 Blythswood St. (at Sauchiehall St.).* ☎ *0141/332-4027. www.billcliffegallery.com. MC, V. Underground: Buchanan St.*

Books

★ Caledonia Books WEST END One of the few remaining secondhand and antiquarian shops in the city of Glasgow. Charming and well run with diverse stock and large sections devoted to Scottish literature, art, natural history, and philosophy. *483 Great Western Rd.* ☎ *0141/334-9663. www.caledoniabooks.co.uk. MC, V. Underground: Kelvin Bridge.*

Voltaire & Rousseau WEST END This shop in an out-of-the-way location near the River Kelvin claims to be the longest running secondhand book store in the city. Tomes are literally piled high. If you do find this place, you might as well visit nearby **Thistle Books** (61 Otago St.; ☎ *0141/334-8777). 18 Otago Lane (near Gibson St.), West End.* ☎ *0141/339-1811. MC, V. Underground: Kelvinbridge.*

Clothing & Fashions

★ Cruise MERCHANT CITY   Bring your credit cards and prepare to spend big for the best selection of designer togs in town. Labels include Prada, Armani, and Dolce&Gabbana. *180 Ingram St. (at the Italian Centre), Merchant City.* ☎ *0141/572-3232. www.cruise fashion.co.uk. AE, MC, V. Underground: Buchanan St.*

Dresses at Felix & Oscar.

★ **Jigsaw** MERCHANT CITY
Housed under the glorious dome of
the Baroque former Savings Bank of
Glasgow, this branch of the fashionable UK chain sells stylish clothes for
women and juniors as well as accessories. *177 Ingram St. (at Glassford
St.).* ☎ *0141/552-7639. www.jigsaw-
online.com. AE, MC, V. Underground:
Buchanan St.*

★ **Mr. Ben** SALTMARKET   Retro
fashions from this shop regularly
appear on newspaper style pages.
Expanded from its originally
cramped premises, it nevertheless
remains chock-full of racks, with an
emphasis on 1960s and 1970s

styles. *101 King St.* ☎ *0141/553-
1936. www.mrbenretroclothing.com.
MC, V. Train: Argyle St.*

★ **Starry Starry Night** WEST END
This shop normally stocks an assort-
ment of antique and vintage clothing.
Also available are secondhand kilts
and matching attire. *19 Dowanside
Lane (off Ruthven Lane).* ☎ *0141/
337-1837. MC, V. Underground:
Hillhead.*

Urban Outfitters COMMERCIAL
CENTER   Founded in 1970, Urban
Outfitters operates more than 130
stores in the United States, Canada,
and Europe, all of which carry a bal-
ance of metro-retro, kitsch, and chic
clothing. *157 Buchanan St. (at Nelson Mandela Sq.).* ☎ *0141/248-
9203. www.urbn.com. AE, MC, V.
Underground: Buchanan St.*

Department Stores
★ **House of Fraser** COMMERCIAL
CENTER   Glasgow's landmark
department store and the place to
head for a wide choice of fashion,
perfume, jewelry, and gifts spread
over several floors and annexes. *45
Buchanan St. (at Argyle St.).* ☎ *0870/
160-7243. AE, MC, V. www.houseof
fraser.co.uk. Underground: St. Enoch.*

★ **John Lewis** COMMERCIAL CEN-
TER   Quality brand names, assured
service, and a 'few-questions-asked'
return policy on damaged or faulty
goods: This makes John Lewis a step

Flea Market Extraordinaire

If you're in Glasgow over a weekend and love flea markets,
then check out the stalls at the weekend ★ **Barras Market,** on
London Road (www.glasgow-barrowland.com; bus: 40, 61, or 62) in
the city's East End. You'll find loads of junk for certain, but you never
know what bargain or collectible might be discovered.

above. *Buchanan Galleries, 220 Buchanan St.* ☎ *0141/353-6677. www.johnlewis.com. AE, MC, V. Underground: Buchanan St.*

Gifts

★★ Felix & Oscar WEST END An offbeat, fun shop for toys, kitschy accessories, fuzzy bags, and a selection of T-shirts that you're not likely to find anywhere else. *459 Great Western Rd.* ☎ *0141/339-8585. www.felixandoscar.co.uk. MC, V. Underground: Kelvin Bridge.*

★ Glasgow School of Art Shop COMMERCIAL CENTER This basement gift and artist supply shop prides itself on its stock of books, stationery, glassware, and jewelry inspired by Mackintosh. It also displays and sells unique artwork by local talent. *11 Dalhousie St.* ☎ *0141/353-4526. www.gsa.ac.uk/shop. MC, V. Underground: Cowcaddens.*

Kilts & Tartans

Geoffrey (Tailor) Kiltmakers COMMERCIAL CENTER Both a retailer and a manufacturer of tartans, which means they have all the clans and sell their own range of

Geoffrey (Tailor) Kiltmaker sells both historic and original tartans.

21st-century-style kilts. *309 Sauchiehall St.* ☎ *0141/331-2388. www. geoffreykilts.co.uk. AE, MC, V. Underground: Cowcaddens.*

James Pringle Weavers COMMERCIAL CENTER In business since 1780, this shop is best known for traditional clothing in the mode of bulky wool sweaters, as well as some more unusual items such as tartan nightshirts. *130 Buchanan St.* ☎ *0141/221-3434. MC, V. Underground: Buchanan St.*

Music

★ Avalanche COMMERCIAL CENTER Rather a compact shop but those-in-the-know flock here to find the latest releases by everybody from the Decemberists to Glasgow faves Sons and Daughters. *34 Dundas St. (near Queen St. Station).* ☎ *0141/332-2099. www.avalanche glasgow.co.uk. MC, V. Underground: Buchanan St.*

★★ Monorail MERCHANT CITY Located within the vegan restaurant and bar, Mono (see p 143), this is the most individual of the independent CD outlets in the city. *10 King St.* ☎ *0141/553-2400. www. monorailmusic.com. MC, V. Underground: St. Enoch.*

Shoes

SoleTrader COMMERCIAL CENTER Particularly popular with trainer enthusiasts, SoleTrader stocks a fashion-conscious selection of European designers and makers, including Birkenstock and Paul Smith. *164a Buchanan St. (at Dundas Lane).* ☎ *0141/353-3022. www.soletrader. co.uk. AE, MC, V. Underground: Buchanan St.*

Nightlife & A&E in Glasgow

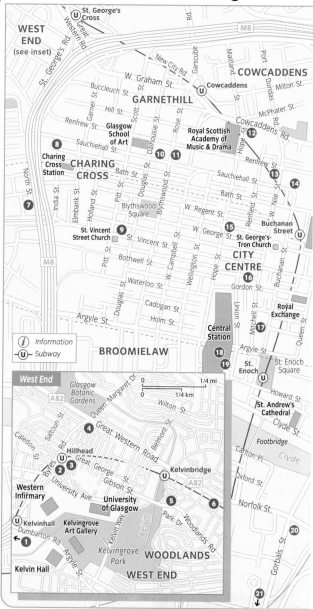

ABC 10
The Arches 18
Babbity Bowster 25
Bar 10 17
Barrowland 31
Bennets 23
Blackfriars 26
Bon Accord 7
Brel 2
Cineworld Renfrew Street 13
Citizens Theatre 20
The City Halls 24
Glasgow Film Theatre 11
Glasgow Royal Concert Hall 14
Grosvenor 3
Heraghty's Free House 21

The Horse Shoe 16
Jongleurs Comedy Club 28
King Tut's Wah Wah Hut 9
Liquid Ship 6
Lismore Bar 1
Nice 'n' Sleazy 8
Oran Mor 4
The Pot Still 15
Revolver 22
St. Andrew's in the Square 30
The Scotia Bar 29
The Stand 5
The Sub Club 19
Theatre Royal 12
Tron Theatre 27
WEST 32

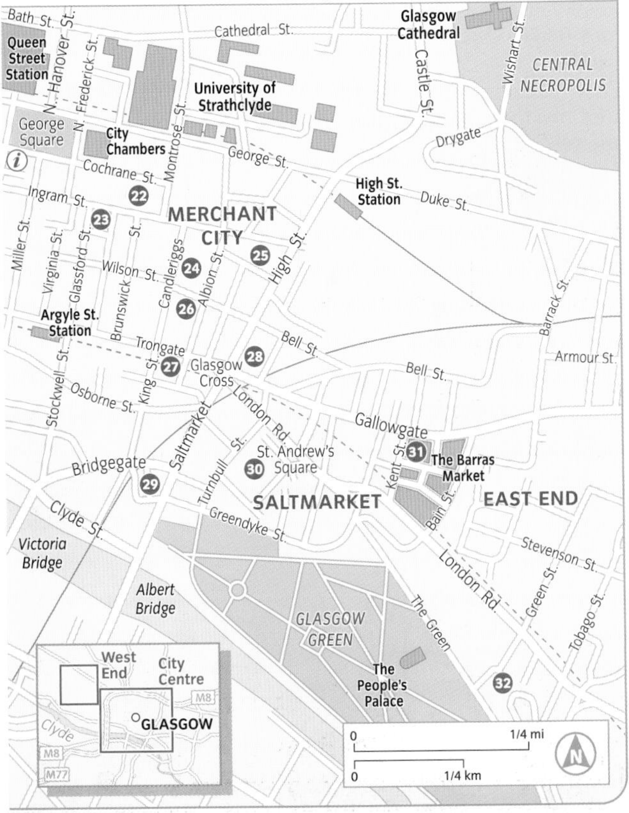

Nightlife/A&E Best Bets

Best for Real Ales
Bon Accord, 153 North St. (p 161)

Best Irish Bar
★ Heraghty's Free House, 708 Pollokshaws Rd. (p 161)

Best 'Palace Pub'
★★ The Horse Shoe, 17 Drury St. (p 161)

Best Whisky Bar
★ The Pot Still, 154 Hope St. (p 162)

Best Micro Brewery
★ WEST, Templeton Building, Glasgow Green (p 162)

Best Dance Club
★★ The Sub Club, 22 Jamaica St. (p 163)

Best for Contemporary Drama
★★ Tron Theatre, 63 Trongate (p 164)

Best Classic Theatre/Opera House
★★★ Theatre Royal, 282 Hope St. (p 164)

Best Independent Cinema
★★★ Glasgow Film Theatre, 12 Rose St. (p 162)

Best Concert Hall
★★ The City Halls, Candleriggs (p 162)

Best Rock Venue
★★★ Barrowland, 244 Gallowgate (p 164)

Best Live Rock Bar
★★ King Tut's Wah Wah Hut, 272 St. Vincent St. (p 164)

Best Juke Box
Nice 'n' Sleazy, 421 Sauchiehall St. (p 164)

Best for Folk Jam Sessions
★ Babbity Bowster, 16 Blackfriars St. (p 161)

Best Modern Gaelic Bar
Lismore Bar, 206 Dumbarton Rd. (p 162)

Best Bargain Tickets
★★ Citizens Theatre, 119 Gorbals St. (p 164)

Best Gay Venue
Bennets, 80 Glassford St. (p 163)

Best Comedy Club
★★ The Stand, 333 Woodlands Rd. (p 162)

Babbity Bowster is a quiet pub to enjoy a pint of ale, with folk music on Saturdays.

Glasgow Nightlife/A&E A to Z

Bars & Pubs

★ **Babbity Bowster** MERCHANT CITY   A civilized place for a pint, with no piped music to distract you. The wine selection and food are both decent, but the real draw is the live folk music played here every Saturday. *16 Blackfriars St. ☎ 0141/552-5055. Train: High St. Underground: Buchanan St.*

Bar 10 COMMERCIAL CENTER   A real mix of people come to this comfortable, effortlessly fashionable bar located in the city center. Glasgow's original style-bar (20 years old in 2011) designed by Manchester's Hacienda creator Ben Kelly is still feeling sharp. *10 Mitchell Lane. ☎ 0141/572-1448. Underground: St. Enoch.*

Blackfriars MERCHANT CITY Real ales are less plentiful in Glasgow when compared to Edinburgh, but this basic Merchant City pub offers a choice of rotating beers, including some from the Continent. Live jazz, comedy, or club nights feature in the basement space at the weekends. *6 Bell St. ☎ 0141/552-5924. Underground: St. Enoch.*

Bon Accord WEST END   This amiable pub, just west of the city center, is the finest in the city for hand-pulled cask-conditioned real ales from across Britain. *153 North St. ☎ 0141/248-4427. Train: Charing Cross.*

Brel WEST END   Possibly the best drinking option on Ashton Lane, this Belgian-themed pub serves up an excellent selection of Continental bottled and draught beers, alongside typical Flemish cuisine. *39–43 Ashton Lane. ☎ 0141/342-4966. www.brelbarrestaurant.com. Underground: Hillhead.*

Belgium-style bar Brel.

★ **Heraghty's Free House** SOUTHSIDE   An authentic Irish pub that serves up pints of Guinness, as well as lively banter. The styling is traditional, with low tables and benches along the back wall. *708 Pollokshaws Rd. ☎ 0141/423-0380. Bus: 38, 45, or 56.*

★★ **The Horse Shoe** COMMERCIAL CENTER   If you visit only one pub in Glasgow, make it this one. It's the last remaining 'Palace Pub', which introduced large, ornate public houses to the city around the turn of the 20th century. The circular bar is one of the longest in Europe. *17 Drury St. (between Renfield and W. Nile Sts.). ☎ 0141/229-5711. Underground: Buchanan St.*

Liquid Ship WEST END   Given its location, you're most likely to rub shoulders with locals here. Owned by the same people who run Stravaigin (p 143), it is unpretentious, with the main bar up a few steps and a lounge in the basement. *171 Great Western Rd. ☎ 0141/331-1901. Underground: St. George's Cross.*

Lismore Bar WEST END   The Lismore is tastefully decorated to reflect traditional Highland culture, with a superb whisky selection to boot. Scottish and Gaelic music is played Tuesday and Thursday nights. *206 Dumbarton Rd.* ☎ *0141/576-0103. Underground: Kelvinhall.*

★ **The Pot Still** COMMERCIAL CENTER   This traditional pub is the best place for sampling single malt whiskies—you can choose from a huge selection lining shelves that rise up to the ceiling behind the bartender. *154 Hope St.* ☎ *0141/333-0980. www.thepotstill.co.uk. Underground: Buchanan St.*

★★ kids **WEST** EAST END   This Munich-style beer hall (in the 'Doge's Palace') brews its own: The best, freshest lager in Glasgow—perhaps in all of Scotland. Food leans toward Bavarian dishes; during the day families are welcome. *Templeton Building, Glasgow Green.* ☎ *0141/550-0135. www.westbeer.com. Bus: 16, 43, or 64.*

Cinema
★★ **Cineworld Renfrew Street** COMMERCIAL CENTER   This multiplex's screens are dominated by blockbusters and big releases, but a couple are reserved for foreign and independent art house films. *7 Renfrew St.* ☎ *0871/200-2000. www.cineworld.co.uk. Tickets £4.50–£6.50. Underground: Buchanan St.*

★★★ **Glasgow Film Theatre** COMMERCIAL CENTER   Head here for a well-programmed daily output of independent, foreign, repertory, and art house films. *12 Rose St.* ☎ *0141/332-8128. www.gft.org.uk. Tickets £4–£6. Underground: Cowcaddens.*

Grosvenor WEST END   Refurbished and restored, the Grosvenor is possibly the only neighborhood cinema still operating in Glasgow,

with a bar and two downstairs screening rooms decked out with comfy leather chairs. *Ashton Lane.* ☎ *0141/339-8444. www.grosvenorcinema.co.uk. Tickets £2.50–£6.50. Underground: Hillhead.*

Comedy
Jongleurs Comedy Club COMMERCIAL CENTER   A comedy franchise that recently moved into the same premises as Mansion House, a glitzy corporate bar and nightclub (replacing Tiger Tiger). Jongleurs draws a range of comedians, including New York native Aidan Bishop, TV funny woman Catherine Tate, and Ed Byrne. *20 Glasford St.* ☎ *0870/011-1960. www.jongleurs.com. £12 cover. Underground: Buchanan St.*

★★ **The Stand** WEST END   Connected to the Edinburgh venue of the same name, and the city's only purpose-built comedy club, it helped to establish the International Comedy Festival held in Glasgow every spring. *333 Woodlands Rd.* ☎ *0870/600-6055. www.thestand.co.uk. £2–£10 cover. Underground: Kelvin Bridge.*

Concert Halls
★★ **The City Halls** MERCHANT CITY   These small halls, which date

The City Halls are home to the BBC's Scottish Symphony Orchestra.

to the 1840s, are home to the BBC's Scottish Symphony Orchestra and are acoustically superior to the city's larger auditoriums. You can catch anything from the Royal Marine's drumming band to modern jazz here. *Candleriggs.* ☎ *0141/353-8000. www.glasgowcityhalls.com. Ticket prices vary. Underground: Buchanan St.*

★ Glasgow Royal Concert Hall

COMMERCIAL CENTER   This modern music hall is primarily home to the Royal Scottish National Orchestra, which plays its yearly Winter–Spring series and Pops seasons in the main auditorium. Modern acts including David Gray and Echo and the Bunnymen have played here too. *2 Sauchiehall St.* ☎ *0141/353-8000. www.grch.com. Tickets £10–£35. Underground: Buchanan St.*

Dance Club

★★ **The Sub Club** COMMERCIAL CENTER   The city's best-known 'underground' club, with DJs such as the long-standing kings of house, Harri and Dom of Subculture. *22 Jamaica St.* ☎ *0141/248-4600. www.subclub.co.uk. £3–£10 cover. Underground: St. Enoch.*

Gay & Lesbian

Bennets MERCHANT CITY   Self-described as the city's 'premier gay and lesbian nightclub,' this split-level club is the most consistently popular on the gay scene. *80 Glassford St.* ☎ *0141/552-5761. £3–£10 cover. Underground: Buchanan St.*

Revolver MERCHANT CITY   Gay-owned and -operated, this friendly bar is host to the light-hearted Queeraoke on Tuesday night and screenings of musicals and comedy sketches on Sunday afternoons. *6a John St.* ☎ *0141/553-2456. Underground: Buchanan St.*

St. Andrew's in the Square.

Folk Music

★ **Oran Mor** WEST END   An ambitious, award-winning center for the performing arts that includes a whisky bar, restaurant, and brasserie as well as spaces for live music—often but not always in a Scottish folk vein. *Byres and Great Western Rds.* ☎ *0141/357-6200. www.oran-mor.co.uk. Ticket prices vary. Underground: Hillhead.*

St. Andrew's in the Square

EAST END   This sympathetically converted early 18th-century church is the city's venue dedicated to folk, Celtic, and traditional Scottish music. *1 St. Andrews Sq. (off Saltmarket).* ☎ *0141/559-5902. www.standrewsinthesquare.com. Tickets £4–£8. Bus: 16, 18, 64, or 263. See also p 122.*

The Scotia Bar MERCHANT CITY   Opened in 1792 (and arguably the oldest bar in Glasgow), this cozy pub frequently has live music, which includes a good dose of folk, rock, country, and blues. *112 Stockwell St.* ☎ *0141/552-8681. www.scotiabar.net. No cover. Underground: St. Enoch.*

Pop & Rock

★★ **ABC** COMMERICAL CENTER   With room for a crowd of about 1,250, this hall is a fairly intimate venue for watching live bands. The line-up is fairly eclectic, with shows ranging from rockers Sisters of Mercy, to indie band TV on the Radio. *300 Sauchiehall St.* ☎ *0870/ 400-0818. www.abcglasgow.com. Ticket prices vary. Underground: Cowcaddens.*

★★★ Barrowland EAST END
There are no seats, and it generally stinks of beer, but this former ballroom remains the most exciting place in the city to see touring artists—anyone from Texas to Pete Doherty. *244 Gallowgate.* ☎ *0141/ 552-4601. www.glasgow-barrowland. com/ballroom. Ticket prices vary. Bus: 40 or 62.*

★★ King Tut's Wah Wah Hut
COMMERCIAL CENTER   This busy rock bar is popular with the Glasgow music and arts crowd, and is a great place to watch both new bands and the occasional international act. Brit-pop band Oasis were famously discovered here in the early 1990s. *272 St. Vincent St.* ☎ *0141/221- 5279. www.kingtuts.co.uk. Tickets £5–£15. Bus: 40, 61, or 62.*

Nice 'n' Sleazy COMMERCIAL
CENTER   This bar books live acts mostly from the local scene to perform in its dark basement space, which hosts club nights on non-gig nights. The ground floor bar houses the city's best jukebox. *421 Sauchiehall St.* ☎ *0141/333-9637. www. nicensleazy.com. Tickets £5–£10; £3 club nights. Train: Charing Cross.*

Theater

★ The Arches COMMERCIAL CENTER
A contemporary arts complex that stages edgy new plays, alongside Shakespeare, at inexpensive prices. There's also a fairly full schedule of live music, regular dance clubs, and visual art exhibits. *253 Argyle St.* ☎ *0870/240-7528. www.thearches.co.uk. Tickets £4–£10. Underground: St. Enoch.*

The Victorian-styled Theatre Royal.

★★ Citizens Theatre SOUTH-
SIDE   The 'Citz', a symbol of the city's democratic approach to theater, is home to a repertory company and has three performance spaces. Prices are always reasonable. *119 Gorbals St. (at Ballater St.).* ☎ *0141/429-0022. www.citz.co.uk. Tickets £5–£15. Underground: Bridge St. Bus: 5, 12, 20, or 66.*

★★★ Theatre Royal COMMER-
CIAL CENTER   This Victorian-style theater is the home of the ambitious Scottish Opera, as well as the recently ascendant Scottish Ballet. London's *Daily Telegraph* has called it 'the most beautiful opera theatre in the kingdom.' *282 Hope St.* ☎ *0870/060- 6647. www.theatreroyalglasgow.com. Ticket prices vary. Underground: Cowcaddens.*

★★ Tron Theatre MERCHANT
CITY   Housed in part of a 15th-century church, this is one of Scotland's leading venues for new drama. It's used often by local companies, such as the acclaimed Vanishing Point, to debut works that end up on the national and international circuit. *63 Trongate.* ☎ *0141/552-4267. www. tron.co.uk. Tickets £3–£20. Underground: St. Enoch.* ●

Before You Go

When to go

The high summer season brings crowds and higher hotel rates, especially in Edinburgh, while the low season carries the possibility that some historic attractions and rural hotels will be closed during your visit (although it's quieter and cheaper). The best time to see Scotland is between May and September, when the country's geared to receive tourists and the weather's generally warmer (and sometimes drier). All attractions, information centers, hotels, and restaurants—no matter how remote—are open to visitors. The days are longest during this time of year. In Edinburgh, fading sunlight lasts well into the evening.

The Weather

No matter the time of year you visit, chances are slim that you'll make it back home without some Scottish raindrops falling on your head. Have a waterproof coat handy. As far as temperatures go—those don't vary radically. Scotland is reasonably cool year-round, although climate change is raising the average temperature in the country. While a few summer weeks can see temperatures occasionally rise above 80°F (27°C), it's typically no hotter than 72°F (22°C), and quite often around 55°F (13°C). In the coldest months, some subfreezing days can be expected, but you won't encounter the bitter cold of the American Midwest.

Useful Websites

Surf the web and you'll find a host of sites aimed at Scottish visitors, which vary in usefulness. With some, I'm never quite convinced they're updated regularly. For official tourist information on Scotland, go to www.visitscotland.com, although it is arguably most helpful as a hotel reservation service.

Here are some others to look at.

- **www.edinburgh.org**: Information specifically on Edinburgh and the surrounding region.

- **www.seeglasgow.com**: Data on Glasgow and the greater Clyde Valley region.

- **www.historic-scotland.gov.uk**: Information on the historical sites operated by the quasi-governmental organization Historic Scotland.

- **www.nts.org.uk**: Data on the historical sites operated by the voluntary charity, the National Trust of Scotland.

AVERAGE TEMPERATURE & RAINFALL IN EDINBURGH & GLASGOW

	JAN	FEB	MAR	APR	MAY	JUNE
Temp. (°F)	38	38	42	44	50	55
Temp. (°C)	3	3	6	7	10	13
Rainfall (in./mm)	2.2/56	1.6/41	1.9/48	1.5/38	2.0/51	2.0/51

	JULY	AUG	SEPT	OCT	NOV	DEC
Temp. (°F)	59	58	54	48	43	40
Temp. (°C)	15	14	12	9	6	4
Rainfall (in./mm)	2.5/64	2.7/69	2.5/64	2.4/61	2.5/64	2.4/61

Previous page: Robert Fergusson statue, Canongate Kirk.

- **www.rampantscotland.com**: Information on Scottish destinations and history, with lots of links to relevant websites.

- **www.nationalrail.co.uk**: Data on travel by train in Scotland.

Cellphones (mobiles)

International visitors can buy a pay-as-you-go mobile phone at any phone store in Scotland. This gives you a local number and minutes that can be topped up with phone cards that can be purchased at newsagents. O2 and Vodaphone are among the best service networks.

Car Rentals

You can get around Edinburgh (and Glasgow) quite well by foot, buses, trains, and taxis. Nevertheless, all major car-rental agencies are located at both cities' airports. In Edinburgh, **Avis** is on West Park Place, near Haymarket Station (☎ **0870/153-9103**), **Hertz** is on Picardy Place (☎ **0870/864-0013**), and **Thrifty** is at 42 Haymarket Terrace (☎ **0131/337-1319**). In Glasgow, **Avis** is at 70 Lancefield St. (☎ **0870/608-6339**); **Budget** is at 101 Waterloo St. (☎ **0800/212-636**); and the leading local company, **Arnold Clark,** has multiple locations (☎ **0845/607-4500**).

Getting **There**

By Plane

Edinburgh International Airport (EDI; ☎ **0870/040-0007**, www.edinburghairport.com) is about 10km (6¼ miles) west of the city's center and has become a growing hub of flights within the British Isles, as well as Continental Europe. From Edinburgh Airport, an **Airlink** bus (www.flybybus.com) makes the 30-minute trip to the city center about every 10 minutes during peak times. The one-way fare is £3.50. A taxi will run you for at least £15.

Glasgow International Airport (GLA; ☎ **0870/040-0008**, www.glasgowairport.com) gets more intercontinental flights. It is located at Abbotsinch, near Paisley, about 16km (10 miles) west of the city via the M8. Bus services (www.glasgowflyer.com) run to and from the city center frequently. The ride takes about 20 minutes (longer at rush hour) and costs £4 for a single fare. A taxi into the city will cost you about £17.

Another option is **Prestwick International Airport** (PRA; ☎ **0871/223-0700**, www.glasgowprestwick.com), which is favored by some of the low-budget airlines such as **RyanAir.** Prestwick's on the railway line to Ayr, and about a 45-minute ride from Glasgow's Central Station. The train fare to Glasgow costs around £6.

By Car

If you're driving north to Scotland from England, there are a couple of options. Take the M1 motorway north from London. Near Newcastle-upon-Tyne, join the A696, which becomes A68 for a final run north into Edinburgh. Alternatively, take the M1 to the M6 near Coventry. Continue north on M6 to Carlisle. After crossing into Scotland, it becomes the M74 heading toward Glasgow. The M8 freeway links Glasgow and Edinburgh.

By Train

From England, two main rail lines link London and Scotland. The faster route traditionally has run between London's King's Cross Station and Edinburgh's Waverley, going by way of Newcastle. The other line connects London's Euston Station and Glasgow Central, passing through Carlisle. Expect the trip to take at least 4½ hours. Fares can vary rather wildly. Call ☎ 0845/748-4950 or head online to **www.national rail.co.uk** for timetable and fare information.

By Bus

The journey from London (coaches depart from Victoria Coach Station) to Edinburgh or Glasgow can take 8 to 10 hours. **Scottish Citylink** (☎ **0870/550-5050;** www.citylink. co.uk) has regular service to Edinburgh. **National Express** (☎ **0870/ 580-8080;** www.nationalexpress. com) runs buses to Glasgow. Fares vary considerably depending on the route you choose, when you buy your ticket, and when you're traveling.

Getting **Around**

By Public Transportation

Edinburgh has an extensive bus network with a fare system that is fairly straightforward. Bus drivers will sell tickets but not give change, so try and always have the correct amount of cash ready when you board. Prices depend on the distance traveled, with the adult one-way (single) fare of £1.30 adult/70p kids covering the central Edinburgh districts. If you plan multiple trips in 1 day, purchase a **Dayticket** that allows unlimited travel on city buses for £3.20 adult / £2 kids. For transport information, contact **Lothian Buses** (☎ **0131/555-6363;** www.lothian buses.co.uk).

Glasgow's bus routes, overseen but not run by **Strathclyde Partnership for Transport** (☎ **0141/ 332-6811;** www.spt.co.uk) can be quite confusing. Local riders know their fares and simply shout it out as they alight. For the rest of us, it feels as if the drivers often make up the price as they go along. Luckily, for most central destinations, Glasgow's circular Underground (officially called 'the Subway' in American fashion) works out best.

The one-way subway fare is £1.20 adult/60p kids. Additionally, there is a reliable commuter/city-suburb train service that crosses the city in several directions (£2.50–£6 round-trip).

By Taxi

Metered taxis are the so-called Fast Black, just like in London, which you can hail or pick up at taxi ranks in the major city centers. Expect to pay at least £5 for a trip across Edinburgh or Glasgow. Surcharges are often imposed for early-morning and late-night runs. Taxis are too expensive to be used for city-to-city travel within Scotland; renting a car or taking the train or bus is cheaper.

On Foot

If you are in shape, this is the best way to get around central Edinburgh, most of Glasgow, and most Scottish towns and villages. Drivers in the major cities can be a bit aggressive, however, so exercise caution before crossing any street. Remember, in Scotland you drive on the left, so you generally must look to your right first before crossing.

Edinburgh Festivals in 24 hours

With different festivals taking place over August, making decisions can seem a bit daunting. There's no reason for it though; here's your quick guide on how to make the most of the Edinburgh Festivals.

- Early morning—start with seeing a reading by one of the many world-famous authors appearing at the Book Festival.
- Late morning—head to the Fringe's half-price hut to see what deals are going. Everyday the hut selects a few shows (from the well-known to the smaller productions) for you to pick from; a good way to navigate your way through the thousands of performances on offer.
- Lunchtime—the great and the good of jazz and blues come to the city in early August. If it's a weekend, catch one of the afternoon bills (some of them free) in various locations across town. If not a weekend then head to one of the 50-plus exhibitions put on by the Art Festival, a growing force in the visual arts scene.
- Afternoon—the International Festival programs the best in theater, dance, opera, and music from all over the world. Catch one of their productions.
- Nighttime—don't miss the larger-than-life entertainment staged at the Castle Esplanade by the Royal Edinburgh Military Tattoo. Military bands from all over the world come to Edinburgh for a spectacle of parades, music, and legendary fireworks on Saturdays.

By Car

Parking is expensive, and restricted to residents in some neighborhoods. There are lots of one-way boulevards, and streets change their names without warning. And the expense of gas (petrol) must be factored into the driving equation as well.

Fast **Facts**

ATMS/CASHPOINTS The easiest and arguably the best way to get cash away from home is from an ATM (automated teller machine), or *cashpoint* as they are commonly called in Scotland. Expect your bank back home to extract a nominal charge for using overseas ATMs.

The **Cirrus** (☎ 0800/424-7787; www.mastercard.com) and **PLUS** (☎ 0800/843-7587; www.visa. com) networks span the globe; look at the back of your bank card to see which network you're on, then call or check online for ATM locations in Scotland.

CURRENCY EXCHANGE You can exchange money anywhere you see a bureau de change sign: ,mainly travel agencies, banks, post offices, and tourist information offices. All will charge some type of commission. Many hotels also offer currency exchange, but their rates are likely to be unfavorable. Your best bet is to withdraw cash from ATMs.

CUSTOMS The same rules for travel to any part of the UK apply to Scotland. Visitors from outside the European Union can bring in for their own use, without paying tax or duty, 200 cigarettes, or 100 cigarillos, or 50 cigars, or 250 grams of smoking tobacco; 4 liters of still table wine and 16 liters of beer; 1 liter of spirits or strong liqueurs or 2 liters of fortified wine; and £350 worth of all other goods, including gifts, purfume and souvenirs. Any amounts over these limits should be declared.

For up-to-date information on customs, see **www.hmrc.gov.uk** and search for 'information for travelers.'

DENTISTS & DOCTORS See 'Emergencies,' below.

DINING It never hurts to make a reservation at local restaurants, as many people do as a matter of habit. It is positively a requirement at the best restaurants on weekends. In general, people don't eat out as late as you will find in Southern European countries. By 10pm many restaurants will no longer be taking orders. Exceptionally few restaurants, if any these days, have dress codes (although shirts and shoes tend to be basic requirements).

DRUGSTORES Drugstores are called pharmacies or chemists in Scotland. If you're visiting from North America, the rules for over-the-counter and prescription drugs will be different and you may not find your preferred brands. Consider bringing what you need with you. Call the NHS (see 'Emergencies,' below) in emergencies.

ELECTRICITY The electric current in Scotland is 240 volts AC, which is different from the US current, so small appliances brought from the US, such as hair dryers and shavers, may not work (and the current will cause damage). If you're considering bringing your laptop, check the voltage first to see if it has a range between 110v and 240v. If the voltage doesn't have a range, the only option is to purchase an expensive converter. If the voltage falls within the range, then you still need to buy an outlet adapter because your prongs won't fit in Scottish sockets.

EMERGENCIES For any emergency, contact the police or an ambulance by calling ☎ 999 from any phone. You can also call the **National Health Service Helpline, ☎ 0800/ 224-488,** which offers health-related advice and assistance from 8am to 10pm daily. If you must seek emergency help at a local hospital, the treatment will be free, although you will be billed for long stays.

EVENT LISTINGS The best source of event listings is a magazine called, appropriately, **_The List_** (www.list. co.uk). Similar in format to London's _Time Out,_ it is published every other Wednesday and is available at major newsstands in Edinburgh and Glasgow.

FAMILY TRAVEL Scotland could be more family-friendly. Some pubs cannot, by law, allow kids; some restaurants, by choice, limit how late in the day families are welcomed. But most historical attractions do offer discount family tickets. When booking hotel rooms, ask whether family suites are available. Look for items tagged with a 'kids' icon in this book.

GAY & LESBIAN TRAVELERS For advice, call the **Lothian Gay and Lesbian Switchboard** (☎ **0131/556-4049**) or the **Strathclyde Gay and Lesbian Switchboard** (☎ **0141/847-0447**).

HOLIDAYS There are several 'bank holidays' in Scotland. In addition to national ones—primarily Christmas, Boxing Day (Dec 26), New Year's Day, Good Friday, Easter Monday, the first and last Mondays in May, and the first Monday in August— some local areas observe their own holidays as well.

INTERNET ACCESS Scottish cities and large towns have Internet cafes, while public libraries have terminals, too. **Easyinternet** (www.easy internetcafe.com) operates cybercafes in Edinburgh and Glasgow. Fees vary, but expect to pay £1 for a half-hour. Increasingly, hotels and guesthouses have computer terminals that offer Internet access.

MONEY Europe's common currency, the euro, isn't used in Scotland. A huge debate once raged among UK politicians over trading the British pound sterling in for the euro—and the pound won. An independent Scotland would probably accept the euro more quickly than the UK as a whole, but nobody expects full Scottish autonomy anytime soon. Though the currency in Scotland is the pound, the notes are different than in England, featuring Scottish historical figures rather than Queen Elizabeth II. Be careful if you travel to England with Scottish bank notes. They're often not accepted by shops and restaurants, where employees are unaccustomed to seeing Scottish bank names on the paper currency.

NEWSPAPERS & MAGAZINES Published in Glasgow since 1783, the **Herald** is one of two major morning newspapers with local news, some international coverage, business reports, comments, sports, and cultural reviews; **The Scotsman** of Edinburgh, published since 1817, is the other. The **Scottish Daily Record** is for tabloid enthusiasts only. To get a less provincial view, buy one of the quality London papers, such as **The Guardian**, although they have limited coverage of Scottish events.

PASSPORTS All US citizens, Canadians, Australians, New Zealanders, and South Africans must have a valid passport to enter Scotland. No visa is required. An immigration officer may also want proof of your intention to return to your point of origin (usually a round-trip ticket) and visible means of support while you're in Scotland. For those who will require a visa: At press time, the UK was considering granting only 3-month automatic visas (replacing 6-month visas).

SAFETY Like most big cities in the Western world, Edinburgh and Glasgow have their share of crime. Handguns are banned by law, however, and shootings are exceedingly rare. Knives present a problem but one largely confined to youth gangs. Fights occasionally flare up in either city center—and in Glasgow particularly when the city's two big soccer teams (Celtic and Rangers) play.

As a tourist, the most important thing you can do is guard yourself against theft. Pickpockets look for people who seem to have the most money on them and who appear to know the least about where they are. Be extra careful on crowded trains in the big cities and when taking money from ATMs.

SENIOR TRAVELERS Many discounts, called concession rates, are available to seniors, generally those over 65. Even if 'concessions' aren't posted, ask if they're available. Elderly travelers should always

The Savvy Traveler

exercise caution in historic sites, where the ground can be uneven, and on cobbled streets in Edinburgh.

SMOKING Smoking in all enclosed indoor public spaces is prohibited, including all bars and restaurants, which may have designated smoking areas outdoors only.

TAXES See 'VAT,' below.

TELEPHONES The country code for Scotland (like all of Great Britain) is **44**. The Edinburgh city code is **0131** (or just 131 if you're dialing from outside the country). Glasgow's city code is **0141**. To make international calls from Scotland, dial 00 and then the country code, local code, and telephone number. The US and Canadian country code is **1**, Australia is **61**, and New Zealand is **63**. To make a collect call overseas, contact an international operator at ☎ **155**.

If you can't find a local number, directory assistance is available from various services (due to privatization), including ☎ **118-811** or ☎ **118-800** for domestic numbers and ☎ **118-505** for international numbers.

Scotland has pay phones that accept coins and credit cards, although the use of cellphones (called *mobiles*) means you see fewer pay phones. For information on cellphones in Scotland, see p 167.

TIME ZONE Scotland follows Greenwich Mean Time, which is five time zones ahead of Eastern Standard Time in the United States (8 hr ahead of the Pacific Coast). So, when it's noon in New York, it's 5pm in Glasgow. The clocks are set forward by 1 hour for British summer time in late March, which expires at the end of October. The high latitude blesses the country with long days in the summer, with sunset as late as 10 or even 11pm. But the opposite is true in winter, when the sun sets as early as 3:30 or 4pm.

TOILETS Public toilets are not quite extinct, but the pattern across the country, in order for councils to save money, is their closure. In the cities, public toilets are usually manned and cost 20p. In country towns and villages they may not have any attendants. Generally speaking, the facilities are clean, but as with so many things, vandalism is not uncommon. Generally, all visitor information centers and tourist attractions have free restrooms.

TOURIST OFFICES In Edinburgh, the **Information Centre** is on Princes Street atop the Princes Mall near Waverley Station (☎ 0131/473-3800 or ☎ 0845/225-5121; www.edinburgh.org). It can give you sightseeing information and also arrange lodgings. The center sells bus tours, theater tickets, and souvenirs of Edinburgh. It also has racks and racks of free brochures. It's open year-round, and hours vary from month to month. In summer you'll find the office open Monday through Saturday from 9am to 7pm and Sunday from 10am to 7pm. In Glasgow, the **Greater Glasgow and Clyde Valley Tourist Board** (☎ **0141/204-4400**; www.seeglasgow.com) is at 11 George Sq. in the heart of the city. In addition to piles of brochures, there are a small book shop, bureau de change, and hotel reservation service. During peak season it is open Monday to Saturday from 9am to 7pm and Sunday from 10am to 6pm. Hours are more limited during winter months.

TRAVELERS WITH DISABILITIES Many Scottish hotels, museums, restaurants, and sightseeing attractions have wheelchair ramps and toilets that are accessible. Recent changes in Scottish law have also put the onus on all new premises to have wheelchair accessibility. At historical sites, however, and in older buildings, access can be limited. Also, not all public transport is accessible for travelers with disabilities.

For assistance and advice, contact **Capability Scotland** (☎ **0131/ 313-5510;** www. capability-scotland. org.uk).

VAT   A consumption tax (20% in 2011) is assessed on pretty much all goods (excepting food) and services. It's called the VAT (value-added tax), and it is calculated like local sales taxes are in the United States, although it is always included in the sticker price. Non-EU tourists are entitled to a refund, which may be significant on large buys. When you make your purchase at a participating retailer (look for signs saying tax free shopping),

show your passport and ask for a tax refund form. Fill out the form and keep any receipts. When you leave the UK, submit the form to Customs for approval.

Once Customs has stamped it, there are various ways to recover the tax. You can mail the form back to the shop and arrange repayment by mail. Some shops are part of networks run by commercial refund companies, whom you later contact for a refund, although an administration fee may be charged. *Note:* If you are going on to another EU country, the scheme doesn't work; you must be leaving the EU zone.

VAT is nonrefundable for services such as hotels, meals, and car rentals.

WEATHER   For weather forecasts and severe weather warnings, contact the **Met Office** (☎ **0870/900- 0100;** www.metoffice.gov.uk).

A Brief **History**

6000 B.C.   Earliest known residents of Scotland establish settlements on the Argyll peninsulas.

3000 B.C.   First Celtic tribes invade, making the use of Gaelic widespread.

A.D. 90   Romans abandon any hope of conquering Scotland, retreating to England, behind the relative safety of Hadrian's Wall.

400–600   Celtic 'Scots' from Ireland introduce Christianity; the Dalriadic kingdom in western Scotland begins.

563   St. Columba establishes a mission on Iona.

1100s   King David I's rule establishes royal burghs and abbeys,

consolidating royal power and importing Norman values.

1270   Birth of William Wallace, key patriot in deflecting the forces of Edward I of England, who wishes to conquer Scotland.

1295   The 'Auld Alliance' between Scotland and France begins.

1306–28   King Robert the Bruce leads an open rebellion against England, which is forced to recognize Scotland's sovereignty at the Treaty of Northampton.

1413   University of St. Andrews founded.

1424   James I is crowned, starting the royal Stuart line in Scotland.

1560s–80s The Reformation establishes a new national religion and the Catholic Mary Queen of Scots is executed in 1587 on orders of her cousin, Queen Elizabeth I of England.

1603 Mary's son, King James VI of Scotland, also accedes to the throne of England as James I, unifying the crowns.

1707 The political and economic union of England and Scotland occurs; the Scottish Parliament is dissolved.

1745 Bonnie Prince Charlie leads a Jacobite rebellion, ending in defeat at the Battle of Culloden (1746).

1750–1850 The Scottish Enlightenment and rapid industrialization transform urban Scotland, while the Clearances strip many of their farms, fomenting bitterness.

LATE 1800s Astonishing success in the sciences propels Scotland into the role of international arbiter of industrial know-how.

MID-1900s The decline of traditional industries (especially shipbuilding) intensifies—redefining the Scottish economy.

1970 The discovery of oil and natural gas in the North Sea brings new vitality to Scotland.

1973 Scotland, as part of the United Kingdom, becomes part of the Common Market.

1997 Scotland passes a referendum to form a new Parliament and create greater self-rule.

1999 Elections for the first Scottish Parliament in almost 300 years are held.

2004 The expensive and much delayed new Parliament building opens in Edinburgh.

2007 The Scottish Nationalist Party, which favors complete independence from England, forms its first government in Scotland.

Scots Language

Glasgow, in particular, has its own vernacular, patter, and words adopted from the Lowland Scots language, once commonly spoken, and other influences. Here is a glossary of some typical words and expressions you may hear on your visit.

blether	chat or gossip
crabbit	grumpy
dinnae	don't or didn't
dreich	drizzly weather
howff	meeting place or pub
messages	groceries or the shopping
neep	turnip
peely wally	pale
scunnered	fed up
steamin'	inebriated
stramash	disturbance
stushie	fuss
wheesht	be quiet

Toll-Free Numbers & Websites

Airlines

AIR FRANCE
☎ *800/237-2747 (in US)*
☎ *800/375-8723 (in US and Canada)*
☎ *0870/142-4343 (in UK)*
www.airfrance.com

AMERICAN AIRLINES
☎ *800/433-7300 (in US and Canada)*
☎ *0207/365-0777 (in UK)*
www.aa.com

BMI BABY
☎ *0871/224-0224 (in UK)*
☎ *870/126-6726 (in US)*
www.bmibaby.com

BRITISH AIRWAYS
☎ *800/247-9297 (in US and Canada)*
☎ *0870/850-9850 (in UK)*
www.british-airways.com

CONTINENTAL AIRLINES
☎ *800/523-3273 (in US and Canada)*
☎ *0845/607-6760 (in UK)*
www.continental.com

DELTA AIR LINES
☎ *800/221-1212 (in US and Canada)*
☎ *0845/600-0950 (in UK)*
www.delta.com

EASYJET
☎ *870/600-0000 (in US)*
☎ *0905/560-7777 (in UK)*
www.easyjet.com

NORTHWEST AIRLINES
☎ *800/225-2525 (in US)*
☎ *0870/0507-4074 (in UK)*
www.flynaa.com

UNITED AIRLINES
☎ *800/864-8331 (in US and Canada)*
☎ *0845/844-4777 (in UK)*
www.united.com

VIRGIN ATLANTIC AIRWAYS
☎ *800/821-5438 (in US and Canada)*
☎ *0870/574-7747 (in UK)*
www.virgin-atlantic.com

Car-Rental Agencies

ALAMO
☎ *800/GO-ALAMO (800/462-5266)*
www.alamo.com

AUTO EUROPE
☎ *888/223-5555 (in US and Canada)*
☎ *0800/2235-5555 (in UK)*
www.autoeurope.com

AVIS
☎ *800/331-1212 (in US and Canada)*
☎ *0844/581-8181 (in UK)*
www.avis.com

BUDGET
☎ *800/527-0700 (in US)*
☎ *0870/156-5656 (in UK)*
☎ *800/268-8900 (in Canada)*
www.budget.com

DOLLAR
☎ *800/800-4000 (in US)*
☎ *800/848-8268 (in Canada)*
☎ *0808/234-7524 (in UK)*
www.dollar.com

ENTERPRISE
☎ *800/261-7331 (in US)*
☎ *514/355-4028 (in Canada)*
☎ *0129/360-9090 (in UK)*
www.enterprise.com

HERTZ
☎ *800/645-3131*
☎ *800/654-3001 (for international reservations)*
www.hertz.com

NATIONAL
☎ *800/CAR-RENT (800/227-7368)*
www.nationalcar.com

PAYLESS
☎ *800/PAYLESS (800/729-5377)*
www.paylesscarrental.com

THRIFTY
☎ *800/367-2277*
☎ *918/669-2168 (international)*
www.thrifty.com

Major Hotel & Motel Chains

BEST WESTERN INTERNATIONAL
☎ *800/780-7234 (in US and Canada)*
☎ *0800/393-130 (in UK)*
www.bestwestern.com

COMFORT INNS
☎ *800/228-5150*
☎ *0800/444-444 (in UK)*
www.ChoiceHotels.com

CROWNE PLAZA HOTELS
☎ 888/303-1746
www.ichotelsgroup.com/crowneplaza

DAYS INN
☎ 800/329-7466 (in US)
☎ 0800/280-400 (in UK)
www.daysinn.com

HILTON HOTELS
☎ 800/HILTONS (800/445-8667 in US and Canada)
☎ 0870/590-9090 (in UK)
www.hilton.com

HOLIDAY INN
☎ 800/315-2621 (in US and Canada)
☎ 0800/405-060 (in UK)
www.holidayinn.com

HYATT
☎ 888/591-1234 (in US and Canada)
☎ 0845/888-1234 (in UK)
www.hyatt.com

INTERCONTINENTAL HOTELS & RESORTS
☎ 800/424-6835 (in US and Canada)
☎ 0800/1800-1800 (in UK)
www.ichotelsgroup.com

MARRIOTT
☎ 877/236-2427 (in US and Canada)
☎ 0800/221-222 (in UK)
www.marriott.com

QUALITY
☎ 877/424-6423 (in US and Canada)
☎ 0800/444-444 (in UK)
www.QualityInn.ChoiceHotels.com

RADISSON HOTELS & RESORTS
☎ 888/201-1718 (in US and Canada)
☎ 0800/374-411 (in UK)
www.radisson.com

RAMADA WORLDWIDE
☎ 888/2-RAMADA (888/272-6232 in US and Canada)
☎ 0808/100-0783 (in UK)
www.ramada.com

SHERATON HOTELS & RESORTS
☎ 800/325-3535 (in US)
☎ 800/543-4300 (in Canada)
☎ 0800/3253-5353 (in UK)
www.starwoodhotels.com/sheraton

THISTLE HOTELS
☎ 0870/333-9292
www.thistlehotels.com

WESTIN HOTELS & RESORTS
☎ 800/937-8461 (in US and Canada)
☎ 0800/3259-5959 (in UK)
www.starwoodhotels.com/westin

Index

See also Accommodations and Restaurant indexes, below.